Strategies and Techniques of Law School Teaching

ASPEN PUBLISHERS

Strategies and Techniques of Law School Teaching

A Primer for New (and Not So New) Professors

Howard E. Katz
Professor of Law
Elon University School of Law

Kevin Francis O'Neill
Associate Professor of Law
Cleveland-Marshall College of Law

 Wolters Kluwer
Law & Business

AUSTIN   BOSTON   CHICAGO   NEW YORK   THE NETHERLANDS

Aspen Publishers
Attn: Permissions Department
76 Ninth Avenue, 7th Floor
New York, NY   10011-5201

To contact Customer Care, e-mail customer.care@aspenpublishers.com,
call 1-800-234-1660, fax 1-800-901-9075, or mail correspondence to:

Aspen Publishers
Attn: Order Department
PO Box 990
Frederick, MD 21705

Printed in the United States of America.

5 6 7 8 9 0

ISBN 978-0-7355-8833-2

Library of Congress Cataloging-in-Publication Data

Katz, Howard E.
  Strategies and techniques of law school teaching : a primer for new (and not so new)
professors / Howard E. Katz, Kevin Francis O'Neill.
    p. cm.
  Includes bibliographical references.
  ISBN 978-0-7355-8833-2 (pbk. : alk. paper) 1. Law—Study and teaching—United States.
2. Law schools—United States. I. O'Neill, Kevin Francis. II. Title.
  KF272.K38 2009
  340.071'173—dc22
                        2009016187

About Wolters Kluwer Law & Business

Wolters Kluwer Law & Business is a leading provider of research information and workflow solutions in key specialty areas. The strengths of the individual brands of Aspen Publishers, CCH, Kluwer Law International and Loislaw are aligned within Wolters Kluwer Law & Business to provide comprehensive, in-depth solutions and expert-authored content for the legal, professional and education markets.

CCH was founded in 1913 and has served more than four generations of business professionals and their clients. The CCH products in the Wolters Kluwer Law & Business group are highly regarded electronic and print resources for legal, securities, antitrust and trade regulation, government contracting, banking, pension, payroll, employment and labor, and healthcare reimbursement and compliance professionals.

Aspen Publishers is a leading information provider for attorneys, business professionals and law students. Written by preeminent authorities, Aspen products offer analytical and practical information in a range of specialty practice areas from securities law and intellectual property to mergers and acquisitions and pension/benefits. Aspen's trusted legal education resources provide professors and students with high-quality, up-to-date and effective resources for successful instruction and study in all areas of the law.

Kluwer Law International supplies the global business community with comprehensive English-language international legal information. Legal practitioners, corporate counsel and business executives around the world rely on the Kluwer Law International journals, loose-leafs, books and electronic products for authoritative information in many areas of international legal practice.

Loislaw is a premier provider of digitized legal content to small law firm practitioners of various specializations. Loislaw provides attorneys with the ability to quickly and efficiently find the necessary legal information they need, when and where they need it, by facilitating access to primary law as well as state-specific law, records, forms and treatises.

Wolters Kluwer Law & Business, a unit of Wolters Kluwer, is headquartered in New York and Riverwoods, Illinois. Wolters Kluwer is a leading multinational publisher and information services company.

Contents

Acknowledgments

The authors would like to thank the many professors—some experienced, some new to the profession—who offered suggestions, feedback, and encouragement, especially Bob Power, Jeff Ferriell, and Randy Barnett. We would also like to thank Kevin's research assistant, Patrick O'Keefe, for his invaluable help.

H.E.K.
K.F.O.

Strategies and Techniques of Law School Teaching

I. Introduction

This book is meant to serve as a resource for new law professors, offering step-by-step, semester-long guidance on building and teaching a law school course. Our advice is by no means basic, and we hope that experienced teachers will find some useful ideas here. Much has already been written about law school teaching.[1] The last several years have seen a burgeoning interest in methods of legal instruction[2] and the design of law school curriculums.[3] A growing number of articles and books discuss innovative classroom methods[4] and assessment techniques[5] — and one report catalogues an impressive array of "best practices" in legal education.[6] There are also many blogs[7] and websites,[8] including an online newsletter,[9] devoted to improving law school instruction.

Why, then, did we bother to write this book? Because most writings focus narrowly on specific teaching techniques or on particular law school courses. Only a few offer general advice to the new teacher.[10] No author, to our knowledge, has ever furnished detailed and comprehensive advice on how to teach a law school course — from choosing a book and designing a syllabus to orchestrating the classroom experience to creating and grading the final exam.[11] That is the aim of this book.

Some overarching themes run through this book. Much of our advice is grounded upon the recognition that law teachers tend to underestimate the enormous barriers to effective communication with their students. It must be borne in mind that your audience is probably not comprised of students who are as gifted as you were.* Ideas or distinctions that you find crystal clear may well be opaque to your students. And the better you know your subject, the greater will be the risk that your students find you unintelligible.** Accordingly, this book will stress the need to be *transparent* with your students — to be open in revealing the structure of your course, identifying key points to be retained from a given lesson, situating the topic you're covering in its larger doctrinal context, and flagging important transitions as you move through the semester.

Other themes flow from this fundamental point. Our emphasis on planning — singling out *in advance* particular goals, topics, and approaches to emphasize in your course — is intended to prevent students from perceiving your presentation as formless and rudderless. We advocate something akin to the "message discipline" successfully employed by modern presidential campaigns.[12] If you attempt to incorporate too many goals, too many topics, too many approaches into your course, you may create the impression that you have no plan at all. Even if you think you're accomplishing more, the likely effect on your students will be to *impede* their capacity to digest what you're throwing at them. Your chances for successful communication will be

---

*   As a first-year student, you may not have been as brilliant as you now remember yourself to have been. It might be edifying if all new professors were required to go back and review the exams they wrote as first-year students.

**   Mastery of a subject is often accompanied by a failure to remember how that subject looks to someone approaching it for the first time.

greatly enhanced if you sit down far in advance of your first classroom session, select a modest number of goals, topics, and approaches, and then focus on those selections throughout the semester.

Throughout this book, we stress the importance of strategy in conjunction with technique. It is easy to think of improvements in teaching as merely adding a few innovations or "tricks" to one's repertoire. We do not underestimate the importance of specific classroom methods,[13] but we try to make the case that prior strategic planning — of *what* you want to accomplish and *how* you'll go about doing it — is just as important as any particular tactic, if not more so. We proceed from the premise that strategy precedes tactics, and tactics precede implementation.

No one reading this book will agree with us all the time. We don't always agree with each other. But we have made a conscious decision to go beyond merely identifying issues, problems, or tensions facing a new law professor. Rather than just exhorting you to "consider X" or "take Y into account," we have expressed our *preferences* — based on personal experience — in situations where there may be more than one way to proceed. If you take issue with how we come down on a particular topic, that's fine. It means that we have flagged an issue needing decision, you have recognized it as an issue, and you have made a conscious choice (either to follow our advice or to go in a different direction). We recognize that "the facts on the ground" are different in every situation — the professor's attributes, the students' characteristics, the institutional norms, and so on. So even if our advice is strongly worded, we never mean to be dogmatic. With each piece of advice, what we're really saying is: "Have you considered the following...?"

Finally, a word about politics. The advice contained in this book can be employed regardless of your ideological perspective and regardless of whether you consciously and overtly teach from that perspective. Our approach neither advocates nor discourages the incorporation of such perspectives as feminist theory, critical race theory, or law and economics. Our principal concern is with effective communication. The *content* of that communication is up to you.[14] We believe that the approach we suggest will enhance your ability to reach your students, regardless of the message you are trying to convey.

II. The Big Picture: Consciously Choosing What Your Course Will Aim to Accomplish

A. THE BROAD RANGE OF POSSIBLE OBJECTIVES

Let's imagine that you've been assigned to teach a basic first-year course — Torts, Contracts, or Property, for example. You're a rookie teacher and your goals are modest. You want your students to learn the material, so you'll march them through the cases in a conventional manner. This seems simple enough — until you start to think about what you want your students to get from your course. Is it only the black-letter rules you want them to learn? Of course not, you say. Nobody strives for just that in teaching a law school class. You also want your students to learn how to *apply* those rules. But is that all? Don't you also want them to see the underlying policies that support the rules? Without an appreciation of policy, their application of the rules may prove mechanical at best, perhaps even heavy-handed or misguided.

Once you think about it, there are many goals that you might want to accomplish in teaching your course. These would include, but are certainly not limited to, the following:

(a) giving your students a strong grasp of the black-letter rules;

(b) teaching them how to apply those rules to new fact patterns;

(c) getting them to see — through problems and hypotheticals — how a seemingly minor change in the facts can produce a change in the outcome;

(d) teaching them case analysis — how to dissect a case, breaking it down into discrete components (facts, issue, precedent, rule, application, holding) in order to discern what the court is actually doing;

(e) honing their ability to distinguish between facts that are pivotal to the outcome of a case and facts that are irrelevant;

(f) getting them to focus on procedural issues — and to recognize that the outcome of a judicial decision must be viewed in terms of its procedural posture;

(g) exposing them to ethical and professional responsibility issues that lurk beneath the surface of the cases;

(h) giving them practical tips on how cases are actually litigated in the real world;

(i) giving them litigation-oriented skills training through courtroom simulations that involve questioning a witness or arguing a motion;

(j) giving them transaction-oriented skills training through contract drafting exercises and mock negotiations;

(k) giving them litigation-oriented drafting exercises (pleadings, motions, jury instructions, etc.);

(l) taking care to include, in your coverage of a given case, the lawyering problems that likely occurred *before* the lawsuit was filed;

(m) teaching your students the methods of statutory construction and giving them statutory drafting exercises;

(n) tracing the historical development of the doctrinal rules in your course;

(o) giving your students an appreciation of the policies upon which the rules are grounded;

(p) covering the larger jurisprudential or philosophical framework of the subject;

(q) developing a coherent theory to explain and justify the rules;

(r) getting your students to examine the subject through a law-and-economics perspective; and

(s) helping them to see the race or gender implications in the rules and cases.

It isn't enough to tell yourself, "Yes, I want all of the above." Nor should you assume that you can accomplish any of these goals simply by marching through the cases in your casebook. To achieve even some of these goals, you'll need to think carefully about how important each one is to you and how it can be accomplished in the classroom. This means consciously allocating class time to achieve your chosen objectives. It means consciously planning how your course will proceed. Every question you ask, every hypothetical you pose, every exercise you perform should be linked to at least one of your goals.

We recommend *telling* your students what your goals are and being transparent in the classroom about what you're trying to accomplish.[15] Since most of your goals will focus on getting your students to develop a certain skill or grasp a certain idea, you're more likely to have success if you tell them what you're seeking. Do not assume that your students already know what you want them to get from your course. Most students are confused about what their professors expect of them and what sorts of skills they are supposed to be developing. First-year students, in particular, are likely to have no idea what you're up to. Many of them will make the faulty assumption that law school is no different from their undergraduate experience. This is why they will doggedly cling to the facts and holding of each case in your casebook — as if they were memorizing the Periodic Table of Elements — but they will draw a blank if presented with a slightly different fact pattern. They simply won't realize, unless you *tell* them, that memorizing cases is not an end in itself — that what you want from them is the capacity to apply what they've learned from those cases to new fact patterns. Once they see what your goals are, once they see what you expect of them, your students will be in a position to adjust their approach to the material. By failing to tell them, you leave them in the dark about what they should be doing — placing them at a disadvantage and hurting your own chances for success. Moreover, if you're transparent about your goals in class, they can better understand why you're asking a certain question or posing a certain hypothetical. They'll perceive you as competent and organized rather than rudderless and obscure.[16]

B. CHOOSING A MANAGEABLE NUMBER OF OBJECTIVES

"Governing is choosing."[17] This remark, by fictional American president Andrew Shepherd, applies just as readily to teaching — because a critical task in designing a course is to choose from a range of possible objectives. In selecting your goals, it is better to take on too few than too many. Especially when teaching a first-year course, it can be time-consuming to achieve even the most basic objectives. Faced with this reality, you should pick a modest number of important goals and spend the semester hammering them home. By attempting to incorporate too many goals, you run the risk that students will perceive your course as a muddled hodgepodge of random thoughts. Our earlier reference to "message discipline"[18] really applies here.

Like the campaign strategists in *The War Room*, you need to pare down the number of "messages" you send in order to ensure that any get through.

When deciding which goals to pursue, take into consideration the unique package of skills and experiences that you bring to the table, your deepest convictions about what your students need most, and your sense of what they are and are not getting from their other teachers. Let's imagine, for example, that you believe very strongly in exposing first-year students to statutory construction and legislative drafting exercises. By talking to the other teachers in your section, you come to find that this is something that your students will be doing in their Criminal Law course. As a result, you are free to cross this off your list of priorities, replacing it with another goal that you might not otherwise have had time to pursue. Maybe you are the only teacher in your section with considerable experience in the courtroom. That might be a reason for including among your goals the teaching of how contract or tort cases are actually litigated in the real world.

When determining the needs of your students, be careful not to confuse *their* situation with *your* situation as a law student. If you are a law professor, it is very likely that you enjoyed law school. It is also likely that the topics and teaching methods that stimulated your interest may not prove equally inspiring to your current students. Just because *you* enjoyed a highly theoretical approach to the material doesn't mean that your students will be equally receptive to it. They might be. But don't assume so. Your main goal should be to teach the course your *students* need — not the one *you'd* most enjoy as a student, and not the one *you'd* most enjoy as a teacher.

One final point about choosing and communicating your goals: Make it clear to your students that they must develop a command of the black-letter rules. All first-year doctrinal classes must deal in some way with the existing rules (though there is probably a course at some hypothetical school — let's call it Yale — where the tort law system or contractual obligations are discussed without reference to any existing rules). It is important to stress to your students that, no matter what else is to be taught and tested in your course, you will expect them to display an absolute command of the rules on your exam. All too often, law professors fail to communicate this expectation, and then, after grading the exams, they express disappointment in the students for failing to discern it and act upon it. The students, meanwhile, are often confused about what is expected of them on the exam. Left unguided, they will make assumptions based on what transpired in the classroom. Since many professors do not devote a great deal of attention to the rules in class (because they assume that it is not a professor's job to go over the black-letter rules), students can get the false impression that the rules are unimportant on the exam. Though law professors will differ about what they are most interested in testing (e.g., application, policy, theory), they will likely agree that students must know the black-letter rules, and that a certain number of points on the exam will hinge on demonstrating that knowledge. If this is true of your course, be sure to tell your students.

C. IMPLICATIONS OF THE CHOICES YOU MAKE

After streamlining and finalizing your list of goals, you need to determine how each goal will be achieved in the classroom and how much time should be allocated to it. Take, for example, your goal of providing practical tips about contract or tort litigation. When and how do you introduce this theme? How frequently will you return to it during the course of the semester? How much time will you devote to it? How much detail will you provide? Will you consciously allocate time to teaching your students how facts are unearthed in the discovery phase, how their truth is tested in the crucible of cross-examination, and how they are illustrated for the jury through demonstrative evidence? Are there passages in your casebook that might provide a fluid transition to some of the practical tips you want to cover? How will you go about conveying this information in the classroom? Will you simply lecture? Will you perform a demonstration? Will you show film clips? Will you get the students involved through role-playing exercises? These are questions that must be answered early on, before you begin to draft your syllabus. Then, as you begin to lay out your syllabus, you will see the opportunities to achieve your objective.

It is essential to remember that you have selected certain goals and discarded others, and that you must remain true to the choices you have made. No matter how tempting it might be, you should resist the urge to incorporate new goals midway through the semester. Doing so will only blur the focus of your course and compromise the time and attention that you had planned to devote to your original goals.[19] As the semester proceeds, we recommend that you jot down observations about how you should teach the course differently the next time through.[20] By maintaining these observations in a file, you can remind yourself about what worked and what didn't work in the classroom and which goals should be added or dropped.

Staying true to your chosen goals is equally important when constructing your exam. You should not feel free to test on policy if you have spent the semester ignoring it. In preparing for your exam, the students will justifiably rely on how you have structured and presented your course. They will focus on the topics and themes that you have focused on. It would be a breach of their trust if you test them to any significant extent on matters that were only peripheral to your basic goals for the course.

When allocating class time for particular goals, remember that dissecting the cases in your casebook is no substitute for teaching your students how to perform legal analysis. These are two different skills.* If you want them to learn how to spot an issue, articulate the governing rule, and apply that rule to the pivotal facts, you'll need to use problems and hypotheticals. This is because students don't view the cases in their casebook as vehicles for learning analytical method. They don't

---

* And there is a third skill worth mentioning here. Skill #1: Pulling the rule out of a case. Skill #2: Applying new facts to an established rule. Skill #3: Comparing two or more competing rules and debating which of them is best. It is useful to highlight for your students at any given time which of these three enterprises they're engaged in. While it may be obvious to you as a professor, it may not be so apparent to your first-year students.

initially see that cases are simply hypotheticals that actually happened, and that the analytical performances by the judges in their casebook are models of what they'll be expected to do on the exam. Even after you get them to see this, they will develop a better grasp of legal analysis by *doing* it rather than merely observing it. All too often, a student's first attempt at legal analysis takes place while writing her first-year exams. This is why those exams are always so disappointing to professors. Their analysis is clumsy and superficial for a reason — because the students haven't spent enough time *practicing* analytical method, let alone getting any feedback on their performance.[21] One way to hone their analytical skills is to conduct classroom exercises in which students are confronted with a short fact pattern and are required to describe exactly what steps they would take in performing their analysis.[22] These sessions can be very helpful to the students if they are scheduled to occur every few weeks — perhaps right after you have finished covering a particular topic. Each time, you can construct the problem so that your students will be applying the black-letter rules and the caselaw they have just learned. In this way, your analytical exercise will double as a review of the substantive rules.

III. Preparing a New Course

A. INITIAL STEPS

Let's imagine that you've just learned from your associate dean that you'll be teaching a course next semester that you've never taught before. What are the first steps you should take?

1. Gaining a Mastery of the Subject: What To Read

Unless you are already very familiar with the subject of your new course, the first thing you should do is to get your hands on a good overview.[23] Why? For two reasons. First, by looking at the subject from a big-picture perspective, you'll start to get some sense of the various topics involved. This will allow you to begin thinking about which topics must be included in your course and which ones may be safely discarded. It will also help you to see how those topics fit together, so that you can plan an order of presentation that is pedagogically sound. Second, by quickly gaining a broad familiarity with your subject, you will be more likely to notice news stories, pending cases, and academic writings that can be gathered as raw materials for your course. This information can escape your attention if you haven't yet grasped the full range of topics embraced by your subject. But once you get a sense of those topics, you'll begin to stumble across all sorts of stories, articles, cases, and illustrations that you can use. The sooner you gain this big-picture perspective, the sooner you'll start noticing and gathering those materials.

Once you've digested an overview of your subject, and once you've reached some tentative conclusions about the topics your course will cover, it's time to gain a more detailed knowledge of the prevailing doctrine, the history of its development, and any current issues in dispute. An obvious source to consult at this point would be the best treatise in the field. A good hornbook will likely contain a lot of detailed rules, some useful history, perhaps some hypotheticals, certainly some indication of unsettled gray areas in the doctrine. At this early stage in your preparation, however, we strongly urge you not to read the hornbook from cover to cover. Instead, glean from it some added detail that will help to fill in your big-picture perspective, but hold back from commencing a minute examination of any particular topic. Until you get into the course, you won't understand the full significance of some of the finer points. Think of yourself as beginning with an aerial view of the entire forest and then descending gradually into the trees. If you fall too abruptly to the forest floor, you'll lose your sense of the lay of the land. At this point, your time is best spent getting a slightly more detailed picture of the topics that will comprise your course — informing yourself to the point where you can make intelligent choices about the next level of readings you'll undertake. Use your hornbook for this limited purpose and then set it aside, to be consulted later when you're learning the finer points and as a companion throughout the semester.[24]

You're ready now to descend another level. Time permitting, you should select some materials that will furnish even more detail. These are law review articles[25] and cases of either a classic or recent vintage. Organize them according to the topics that your course will cover. Armed with the big-picture perspective you've already achieved, you can use these readings to begin mastering your subject.

Don't imagine that you'll be able to digest everything on your reading list before the semester starts. Time flies when you're a professor with a new course to prepare (whether or not you're having fun). So look carefully at the readings you've collected for each topic and set some priorities. Give some thought to whether you should exhaust all the readings for one topic before moving on to the next, or whether your sense of preparedness demands that you skip around so that no topic remains unexamined until the end.

At this stage of your preparation, the key thing to remember is this — by the first day of class, it is more important for you to have determined the topic-by-topic structure of your course than to have mastered every detail, every fine point of your subject. You'll be anxious, of course, to learn as much as you can about your subject before classes commence. But gaining a mastery of your subject is something that you can pursue throughout the semester (and for years to come). By the start of classes, it is much more critical for you to have envisioned the big-picture structure of your course. As you teach it, you don't want the course to be unfolding for you step by step, day by day, without any clear picture of what's around the corner. The very act of organizing your course into discrete topics and then deciding upon a topic-by-topic flow will help *you* to see how the pieces fit together. This will prove very helpful when you are fielding student questions. First, it will aid you in dealing with the many questions that conflate or confuse distinct topics. Second, it will help you to realize that a particular question pertains not to the topic you're currently covering but to a topic that you will address later in the semester. Obviously, if the question applies to a later topic, you'll want to defer discussion. Sometimes a question will relate to both the current and a future topic. If you understand the contours of the entire course, you'll be in a better position to decide whether to tackle that question now or defer it, and you'll be able to point out the connection for future reference.

2. Funneling Ideas and Materials, Topic by Topic, into a Teaching Outline for the Entire Course

What should you do with the "raw materials" to which we referred above? They should be funneled, topic by topic, into a teaching outline for your entire course. Needless to say, this outline should be maintained on a computer, so that it may be easily updated and revised. Begin the outline by creating a major section for each topic to be covered in your course. Add subsections for discrete doctrines or issues that fall within a given topic. Within this skeleton, you should add any insights, questions, explications, illustrations, hypotheticals, or exercises that you conceive or encounter while immersing yourself in the readings described above.[26]

As it takes shape, your teaching outline will become a repository of ideas and devices that you can use in the classroom, organized in accordance with the structure of your course.[27] Individual sections can be moved around to reflect how you have ordered the progression of topics. And within each section, you can arrange the flow of ideas with great precision. Of course you may choose to skip over certain points when you're actually teaching the class. Maybe you're pressed for time that day, or the point will be lost on this particular group of students. But at least the idea is right there to jog your memory, located in the very spot where it's most relevant to your course.

We know of one professor who used to tear up his teaching notes at the end of each semester, preparing them anew the next year. He believed that this kept him fresh in his approach to the material. We have nothing but admiration for someone who can do that. And we agree with his underlying aims — that professors must stay current, must try to see the subject through the eyes of someone who has not yet mastered it, and must avoid marching through the material as if they were on autopilot. But we believe that there is much to be gained by using your teaching notes as an armature on which to build your knowledge, as long as you regularly update and revise them. Over time, this teaching outline will capture and reflect new insights that you've gained from reading or from classroom experiences. For example, suppose a student raises a good question that you didn't anticipate, and it prompts you to provide a clarification that students find helpful. Should you trust your memory to unearth this clarification one or more years from now when you're teaching the course again? Obviously, it would be better to insert it now into your teaching outline, while the details are still fresh in your mind.[28] Maybe you've always had trouble getting your students to grasp a particular distinction — but then, one day in class, you hit upon a hypothetical that makes it clear. To be sure that you remember that hypothetical next time, you'll want to enter it right into the appropriate spot in your teaching outline. Through this gradual accumulation of ideas, your teaching outline will grow richer over time.

3. Using "Shadow Sources"

In the next section, we will discuss how to choose a casebook for your course. That process will require you to examine and compare a number of competing titles. Among the books that don't make your final cut, you'll likely find many good qualities. Maybe one of them offers more detailed coverage of certain topics than the book you chose for your class. Or maybe one of them features excellent problems and hypotheticals, but you rejected it for shortcomings in other areas. We recommend that you retain one of those rejected books and use it as a "shadow source" for your course — i.e., a repository of information, elucidation, questions, problems, hypotheticals, and illustrations, all as a personal supplement to the casebook you selected. Each time your students embark on a new chapter in your casebook, pull out your shadow source and examine its treatment of the same subject. Perhaps it will give you ideas on how to introduce the subject, describe its historical development, illustrate its application, or invite student analysis through problems and hypotheticals.

Your shadow source need not be another casebook — it can be the *teacher's manual* from another casebook. Pressed by publishers, more and more casebook authors have written detailed teacher's manuals. Twenty years ago, such manuals were few and far between, and they tended to offer only the most general advice. Nowadays, a teacher's manual accompanies almost every casebook, and many of them serve as a comprehensive guide. Though they vary widely in quality, these manuals can be a fruitful source of questions, hypotheticals, and illustrations. They can give you fresh ideas for how to approach any cases that your book has in common with the shadow source. A good teacher's manual can even give you food for thought on the larger questions posed by your course. Take, for example, the experience that one of us had in teaching Constitutional Law. He selected the Barron & Dienes casebook,[29] but used as his shadow source the teacher's manual to Farber, Eskridge & Frickey.[30] That teacher's manual provided him with a wealth of ideas, partly because the philosophies behind the two books were different. It gave him a fresh perspective — not only on individual cases, but also on questions of coverage, emphasis, historical context, even the grand themes that run through constitutional law. The fresh perspective furnished by that manual enriched his teaching of the course.

B. CHOOSING A BOOK

We come now to the all-important task of choosing your textbook. This decision looms large because day after day, all semester long, it will constantly affect how you and the students experience your course. The last thing you need is to spend the semester fighting your book — scrambling to chart a coherent path through its poorly organized chapters, apologizing for its paucity of explication, muffling its ideological slant, straining to counteract its needless complexity, struggling to decipher its maddening "notes." Since the stakes are high, you need to commence your search at the earliest possible moment and devote significant time to it. Contact all the legal publishers,[31] tell them about the new course you'll be teaching, and request a complimentary copy of all their offerings in the subject area. Soon you'll be inundated with casebooks.[32] Now begins the process of examining and comparing them. The time and care that you devote to this process will pay dividends for months, even years, to come.

After selecting a book and teaching a whole semester with it, you will find yourself tied to it in hundreds of small ways — and this can discourage you from trying a new book the next time you teach that course. This is because much of what you do each day in the classroom is connected to the text and structure of the book you have chosen. The questions you ask, the issues you identify, the clarifications you provide are often a response to something in your book. In essence, you carry on a semester-long conversation with your book — or, perhaps more accurately, you use specific passages in your book as a springboard for introducing and examining certain points you want to cover. After you have taught the course several times, you develop a strong familiarity with your book — and this can make you reluctant to abandon it,[33] even though you are all too aware of its flaws. At least those flaws are no longer the hidden landmines that would await you in any new casebook you might select. Since you won't readily depart from your original choice, you'll want to make that choice with all due deliberation.[34]

In the subsections that follow, we offer some advice about making that important choice. But before we proceed to that advice, let's pause to consider the extent to which your own faculty may influence your choice. The impact of faculty politics on your book choice will vary widely from school to school. On some faculties, it won't be an issue at all. On other faculties, you may feel pressured to select a particular book. This can happen if someone on your faculty has authored a casebook for your course. It can also happen if one particular book is favored by the other faculty members who teach your course. Every faculty is different, so it will be up to you to gauge how much freedom you have to make an independent choice. Of course it can be *advantageous* to teach out of the same book as one of your colleagues. Throughout the semester, you can go to that person for advice on how to handle particular sections in the book.[35] And this is likewise true if the author of that book is on your faculty. Ultimately, we believe that a faculty colleague's authorship or advocacy of a particular book should be a factor in, but not dispositive of, your choice. Assuming that faculty politics will not force your hand on this question, we recommend that you evaluate every available book on the merits, using the criteria that we have set forth below.

1. Don't Automatically Choose the Most Popular Book, the Most Interesting Book, or the Book That Your Teacher Used

When you have gathered all of the competing casebooks and stacked them upon your desk, you'll be dismayed by how numerous and thick they are — and you'll feel an impulse to curtail the selection process by abruptly making a "safe" choice. To this end, you may find yourself drawn to the best-selling casebook in its field, or the one that is most widely revered, or the one that *your* teacher selected when you took the course in law school. Resist this impulse. Fight the urge to rush your decision. Try to give every book an equal chance.

Just because a book is widely used or highly respected doesn't mean that it will be a good fit for *you*.* Maybe its organizational structure conflicts with your sense of how the topics should be ordered. Maybe its editing of the cases seems heavy-handed. Maybe its notes are more baffling than helpful. Maybe it goes into far more detail than you could ever hope to cover. Or maybe it employs an approach to the subject that you find unfeasible. Let's use this last point as an example. One of us has been teaching Evidence since 1995. His experience as a student left him convinced that reading appellate opinions is no way to learn the rules of evidence — that a problem approach is essential to gaining a grasp of the rules. Years later, when he found himself a professor, this conviction guided his choice of a textbook. Among many competing titles at that time, three books stood out as enormously popular and respected. But each of those books relied heavily on appellate cases, interstitial notes, and law review excerpts as the principal means of teaching Evidence. Notwithstanding their well-deserved acclaim, these books were simply wrong for his course — because they were bereft of problems, and he was committed to using problems every single day in his classroom. So, pushing the best-sellers aside, he turned his attention to the few (and relatively new) books that employed a problem approach.[36] Among these, he was deeply impressed by and finally chose the Mueller & Kirkpatrick book,[37] which was then in only its second edition and just beginning to achieve acclaim.[38] That selection comported with his vision of the course, even though it rejected the pre-eminent titles of the time. The lesson to be learned here is that zeroing in on the most popular or respected book in its field is no short cut to finding the book that is best for you.

Likewise, don't automatically go with the book your own professor used. It can be tempting to pick that book because you already have some familiarity with it. You've seen at least one model of how that book can be organized into a course. And if your teacher was effective, your class notes as a student may be very helpful.[39] But you don't know why your professor chose that book or whether your professor was happy with it. For all you know, your professor abandoned that book the very next year. But let's assume that he or she went on using it. Sticking with one book, even for many years, is not necessarily a ringing endorsement of that book. Law

---

* Moreover, the best-seller is not necessarily the best book to teach from — because pedagogical soundness and student accessibility are not, for many professors, the decisive factors in choosing a casebook.

professors have to invest so much time and effort in building a course around their chosen book that many will not readily switch to a new one, even if they are less than happy with it.[40] Plenty of new casebooks have entered the marketplace in the years since your professor selected that book. You owe it to yourself to examine all the available titles. The best book for the approach you want to take may not have been written yet when your professor made his or her choice. The main advantage of choosing the book your professor used — namely, your class notes — may well be offset by a good teacher's manual accompanying a rival casebook.

Finally, be cautious about selecting the book that you personally find most interesting. Remember — your *students* are the real audience for the book that you're selecting. The book that you find most stimulating may leave your students utterly perplexed. Think about what would cause you to regard a casebook as particularly interesting. Maybe it's because the book delves deeply into one of your favorite topics, lavishing extended treatment upon cases that are too obscure even to be cited in other books.[41] Admittedly, the detailed treatment of that particular topic and the inclusion of those particular cases could be regarded as an encouraging sign that the authors of this book are right on your wavelength. But what about your students? Do *they* need those cases? Do *they* need such in-depth exposure to a topic that other casebooks barely cover? This is the danger of the "interesting" book. It may lack a sense of balance and proportion. Maybe its treatment of this particular topic is part of an overall effort to be *encyclopedic* — furnishing far more detail than you can comfortably handle and saddling you with the type of editing problems that we discuss below.[42] Or maybe it follows each case with pages and pages of "provocative" questions — thought-provoking to you, but opaque to your students.[43] Or maybe it lacks an appropriate sense of emphasis — treating peripheral topics as if they were important, and vice versa. Or maybe it probes the subtleties of its subject in ways that are satisfying to an expert like you, but will be lost on newcomers to the field like your students.[44] In our experience, it is often a mistake to choose a book because it includes a favorite case, or because it strives to be encyclopedic, or because it has an "intellectual depth" that appeals to the scholar in you. Though such a book may initially strike you as intriguing, be careful to ensure that its coverage is balanced and that it maintains an appropriate level of analysis and detail throughout.

2. Don't Base Your Decision on the First Few Chapters of a Book

Faced with the task of comparing so many different casebooks, you'll be tempted merely to examine the first few chapters of each book. This is understandable, but it's a mistake. Sometimes a casebook will get off to a great start only to grow muddled in its later chapters. If you adopt the book without venturing beyond its early chapters, you may be in for a rude surprise. Halfway through the semester, when you're covering an important section of the course, it will seem as if your casebook has been hijacked by new authors. Suddenly the book will be plagued by odd case selections, clumsy organization, or poorly written notes. The same book that you found so impressive in its opening chapters will seem transformed into a liability. Obviously, it's better to uncover those problematic chapters in July, when you're deciding which book to adopt, than in November, when you've got seventy students dissecting that book each night.

Is it really possible for a casebook's quality to veer markedly from chapter to chapter? Yes — particularly with books that have multiple authors. Often different chapters of a casebook are the responsibility of different authors, so that there may not be a uniformity of quality or approach. Thus, no matter how impressed you are by the opening chapters of a given book, do not adopt it until you've examined any subsequent chapters that are critically important to your course.

3. Remember That It's Easier to Add Material Than to Subtract It

Most casebooks include more material than you can comfortably cover in a single course. This is by design — to give each professor flexibility in tailoring his or her course. But it presents problems. If you're new to the subject, you may not have a good grasp of which sections or chapters are the best candidates for omission. All things being equal, then, it is preferable to choose a casebook that is shorter — because you won't have to edit the book as heavily. The more you have to edit a book, the greater will be the likelihood that you give your students a flawed perspective on the subject. If the book omits a case or topic that you believe is important, it's easy enough to *give* that material to your students. But the book that omits nothing can be a real headache to reshape.

Take, for example, the experience that one of us had the first time he ever taught Property. He initially chose the Dukeminier casebook,[45] the most popular title then and now. But that choice proved problematic because he had to teach the entire course in only four semester hours,[46] and Dukeminier is not a compact book. After trimming whole chapters, he found that, even within the topics that remained, the book went into far greater detail than he had time for. The level of detail was more than he would have desired even if he had been given five or six semester hours. At first, he believed that he could edit out chunks of the remaining chapters, either case by case or note by note. This is not something you want to get into if you can avoid it. If you are new to the course, there is a good chance that you will botch the job, eliminating something that's important or throwing the coverage out of balance. Well-edited casebooks tend to avoid redundancy — so if you skip a long case to save time, there may be no other mention of the basic rule that the case was included to illustrate. Now you'll have to *add* something shorter to correct the omission. And the notes that appear on subsequent pages, offering observations that you feel are valuable, may be rendered useless if the lead case is no longer assigned.

Rather than trimming an overly detailed casebook, some professors simply assign all the surplus material, resolving not to spend any class time covering the pages that could have been omitted. This is a serious mistake. First, you are asking the students to read material that you really don't value. That is a breach of their trust. Second, if something falls within their reading assignment, students are going to ask questions about it whether you bring it up or not. Now you're faced with a choice. You can answer those legitimate questions, consuming class time that you had allocated for something else, or you can brush the questions off. The latter tactic sends a clear message to students that not everything you assign is important. And that can undermine their commitment to reading the whole assignment later on, when it really *is* important to you.[47]

Because of these problems, we tend to prefer a more compact book if forced to choose between equally attractive alternatives. By picking a book that is not quite so comprehensive, one that raises slightly fewer subtle points,[48] you at least give yourself the chance to cover it carefully and thoroughly in class. We believe that this is better than choosing a longer and more detailed book, one that must either be trimmed considerably or covered by means of gargantuan reading assignments — vast stretches of text that your students can never fully absorb and that you can only skim in class. In the end, it is easier and safer to supplement a shorter book with cases and articles of your own choosing than to race breathlessly through a longer book or crudely cut it down to size.

4. Is the Book Organized in a Way That Will Confuse Students or Conflict with Your Vision of the Course?

When comparing rival casebooks, one of the first things to focus on is how they organize the material. Take each competing text and scrutinize its table of contents. Are different topics lumped together without adequate demarcation? Are related topics dispersed? Are topics arrayed in a progression that makes them difficult to digest? Do the authors make clever but ultimately strained and unhelpful connections? Do they employ an organizational scheme that obscures current doctrine? Does the book deviate significantly from the traditional organization of the course (as evidenced by the Restatement or by hornbooks and commercial outlines)? If so, is there any advantage to this deviation? And does the gain outweigh the loss? If you have serious concerns about the grouping and ordering of topics in a book, if you feel that the book is organized in a way that will confuse students, or if the structure of that book cannot be reconciled with the structure of your course, you should strongly consider rejecting it. This is because a poorly organized book can undermine your performance of two important tasks: helping your students to see the big picture, and preventing them from blurring discrete topics and doctrines.

Part of being an effective law teacher is helping your students to see the big picture — helping them to form a mental map of the topics that comprise your course.[49] This is hard enough to do even when you are in sync with the organizational structure of your book. But if you have to fight your book's structure, reshaping it through reading assignments that ricochet from chapter to chapter and case to case, your students will have a terrible time seeing how it all fits together. Don't forget that many students *rely* on the structure of their casebook to gain an overarching sense of the subject you're teaching them. Many of them use the book's table of contents as the starting point in creating their course outlines. These tools for seeing the big picture will be lost to your students if you give them a book whose structure you reject.

Students have trouble grasping transitions and distinctions between discrete topics, recognizing the boundary lines between separate but related doctrines. In a poorly organized book, those transitions and distinctions will be blurred, those separate but related doctrines will be lumped together in a congealed mass or shuffled and scattered into several far-flung chapters. In an effort to rectify such problems, you'll be forced to concoct convoluted reading assignments that send your students bouncing all over the book. Even if your syllabus displays those reading assignments with carefully constructed subheadings — all in an effort to make the necessary connections and draw the necessary distinctions — you can never fully overcome the organizational flaws that you inherit from your casebook. It may not be logical, but when a syllabus significantly deviates from the book's own table of contents, students perceive this as confusing — and they will let you know about it in their course evaluations.

5. Is the Book Written from an Ideological or Pedagogical Perspective with Which You're Uncomfortable?

Depending on the subject you're teaching, you may feel it appropriate to expose your students to a generous sampling of ideological and analytical perspectives. Getting your students to look at the law through different lenses — feminist theory, critical race theory, and law and economics, among others — is arguably part of giving them a well-rounded education. But if a casebook manifests a distinct political or ideological emphasis, and you are uncomfortable with that emphasis, you'll want to find a different book. This is because you don't want to spend the semester muffling your authors — suppressing their biases or counteracting their preoccupations.

Likewise, you should scrutinize the competing casebooks to see whether any are written from a *pedagogical* perspective with which you're uncomfortable. Does the book focus too much or too little on theory, too much or too little on history, too much or too little on the black-letter rules? Does it supply an abundance of problems and exercises, or does it feature the conventional montage of cases, notes, and miscellany? Does the book provide long passages of doctrinal explication, or do the interstitial notes contain more questions than answers? Which of the foregoing characteristics *should* a book possess? To answer these questions, you'll have to arrive at some definite conclusions about how law students should be taught and what they need from their casebook. As your students endeavor to distill the black-letter rules, how much help should they receive from their casebook? How deeply should it immerse them in history, theory, or policy? Will they learn best from a problem approach, or will a traditional casebook suffice? By answering these questions clearly and honestly, your own pedagogical perspective will come into focus. Let it guide you during the selection process — and you'll avoid spending the semester in pedagogical conflict with your book.

Here is a concrete example of a pedagogical conflict that can very easily arise. Some books deliberately include a number of cases that were wrongly decided or that represent a minority rule. Some professors welcome the inclusion of such cases, using them as an opportunity to explore a variety of issues.[50] But other professors may strongly oppose the inclusion of wrongly decided or minority-rule cases, having witnessed the abject confusion that such cases trigger in students. If you are pedagogically opposed to the inclusion of such cases, you'll need to screen the available casebooks to identify the offending passages.

If an otherwise promising book falls short of matching your pedagogical perspective, do not automatically reject it — but do recognize that this is a portent of trouble. Adapting the book to your approach may prove a real struggle. Let's say, for example, that you plan to teach your course with a heavy emphasis on problems, but the book you've selected doesn't employ a problem approach. If you like the book enough, you could decide to supply the problems by writing them all yourself.[51] But doing this may be a lot more trouble than the book is worth. First, you will pay a steep price in class preparation time. Though the task may seem manageable in the quiet days of summer when you first undertake it, you will likely be scrambling during the semester to conceive the problems, fashion them into a student-friendly format, and then distribute them (in hard copy or on the Web). Second, given the strain of trying to create a full set of problems during a single semester, you may wind up with a product that is uneven in quality and not well integrated with the other course materials. Had you selected a problem-oriented book in the first place, you probably wouldn't be facing such concerns.[52] Finally, if the book doesn't have the thing you want (problems, in this example), it may be because the book is written from a teaching philosophy that is alien to yours. And this means that when you try to fill the void in that book by creating supplemental materials, the book's divergent teaching philosophy may well clash with your materials, thwarting their integration into your course. Normally, as we've said,[53] it's easier to add to a book than subtract from it. But if you're planning to add problems to a book whose focus or approach is incompatible with yours, the book may prove resistant to the integration of any new materials that you might create.[54]

6. Are You a Long-Case Teacher or a Short-Case Teacher?

When selecting a book, another question to ask yourself is: Are you a long-case teacher or a short-case teacher? Most law professors, whether or not they realize it, fall into one of these two camps. Do you want a book that reprints the cases with very little editing, preserving their factual complexity to allow a deeper look at the underlying characters and events? Or do you prefer a streamlined account, one that trims the procedural history, eliminates the secondary arguments, and condenses or summarizes the facts? It is well worth your time to think carefully about where you stand on this question — because many casebooks reflect a long-case or short-case philosophy.[55] If you select a book whose philosophy conflicts with yours on this question, you will find yourself saddled with a constant source of frustration. A long-case teacher using a short-case book will repeatedly complain that important passages in each case have been edited out. A short-case teacher using a long-case book will be exasperated by having to assign twenty pages "just" to cover one or two rules.

How can you tell whether you're a long-case or a short-case teacher? A long-case teacher would think nothing of spending one or two class sessions on a single case — reviewing its procedural posture, exploring the evidentiary record, dissecting the analytical method employed by the court, perhaps even speculating why that case wound up in court in the first place and how it affected the parties. A short-case teacher will use a case as the setting for a surgical strike — to make a few specific points, to accomplish a few targeted objectives, and then move on. Long-case teachers want their students to be confronted with a richness of factual detail, so that they can learn to separate the relevant from the irrelevant, and to zero in on the facts that are pivotal. Short-case teachers want cases that are stripped down to their essential facts, and they use those cases almost like hypotheticals — to train their students how to identify the issue and apply the governing doctrine to new situations. Short cases lend themselves more readily to variations of the basic fact pattern, which can be used to demonstrate the limits of the doctrine at hand. For long-case teachers, a case is a springboard for exploring a broad range of topics: the real-world aspects of litigating a case, the structuring of arguments to the court, the process of judicial decision making, the impact of political pressures and institutional traditions on the behavior of judges, and any other topic the material might suggest.[56] For short-case teachers, the potential uses of a case are not so open-ended. A case will be used to make one or two doctrinal points, perhaps to situate those points in a larger theoretical or policy perspective, and, before moving on to the next case, to give the students practice applying the rules they've learned.

Consider, for example, the topic of future interests in the first-year Property course. If you want a case that is sufficiently rich in facts that it can serve as a springboard for analyzing the interests of the various family members, for inquiring into their motivations, and for considering the harmful impact of such litigation upon their relationships, all woven into a discussion of the rules, you're a long-case teacher. If you plan to use the case mainly as a vehicle for introducing the rules, allocating the great bulk of your presentation to the rules themselves, with only a passing reference to the foregoing themes (e.g., "These issues often come up in the context of intra-family disputes. . ."), you're a short-case teacher.

If you fall decisively into the long-case or short-case camp, then try to find a book that is compatible with your preference. At the very least, be sure to avoid any book that reflects the extreme opposite perspective.

7. Will Students Find the Text or Notes in the Book to Be Unintelligible?

A good way to antagonize your students is to select a casebook that they will find incomprehensible. Watch out, in particular, for those after-the-case "notes," where the authors emerge from the montage of materials they've assembled and speak directly to the reader. Many authors use these passages not to explain, not to clarify, not to provide historical or doctrinal context, but simply to ask questions. And these questions elicit very different reactions from professors than from students. Professors often regard them as a rich source of ideas, suggestions, and insights, believing that they will stimulate the reader. Most students find them unintelligible — not just unhelpful but downright inscrutable, like the queries of the Sphinx. As they accumulate, these questions can become deeply irritating to the students. Eventually, they stop reading them. And once they have tuned out your book, they won't be all that receptive to you.

Bear this in mind when selecting a book. Try to steer clear of books that are bereft of expository passages, books that will not deign to explain, books that are filled with questions that the authors never even try to answer. Such a book — if *you* find it sufficiently intriguing — might serve you well as a "shadow source,"[57] furnishing raw material that you can reshape into a form that is more accessible to your students. It's better to use a recondite book in this fashion than to foist its obscurity directly upon your students.

Some law professors voice concern that casebooks with *clear* notes leave them with little to do as classroom teachers. We find this implausible. First, we wonder why a teacher would ever prefer obscurity to clarity in selecting a casebook. But even if your casebook *is* guilty of containing many lucid passages, you'll still face the daunting task of teaching your students how to dissect a judicial decision and how to apply its holding to new fact patterns. In accomplishing these objectives, you'll likely be more efficient if the casebook hasn't left your students irritated and bewildered. And that will give you extra time to pursue the secondary goals[58] you've targeted for the course. It is not too much of an overstatement to observe that even if you gave your students a summary and the attendant hornbook excerpts for every case and topic you cover, you could still find plenty of things to discuss in class and plenty of confused students in need of your guidance.

In the modern casebook, you are as likely to find *before*-the-case notes as after-the-case notes — and the former can be just as problematic as the latter. Introductory notes are at their best when they simply set the stage for the case that follows, providing students with historical or doctrinal context and giving them a few basic points to watch for.[59] But some authors try to accomplish objectives with their before-the-case notes that are best reserved for after-the-case notes. For example, zeroing in on the finer points of a lawyer's argument is something best pursued in *after*-the-case notes because the student will not be able to appreciate it until the details of the case are freshly in mind. But some authors make the mistake of loading their introductory notes with so much minutiae or miscellany that their value to the student is lessened. Here, then, is another flaw to be watchful for when selecting a casebook: Does the book contain before-the-case notes that are so clogged with detail or digression that they hinder, rather than enhance, the student's ability to understand the context or significance of the case that follows?

Finally, a word about transitions. We have already stressed[60] that students have trouble recognizing the boundary lines between separate but related topics. Depending on how it is written, a casebook can exacerbate or alleviate this problem. So it is well worth your time, when comparing rival books, to look carefully at how the authors navigate the sensitive interval between the end of one topic and the beginning of the next. An artful transition will point out, where appropriate, any common history or function that unites the adjoining topics. But the most important function of a transition is to draw a clear dividing line between discrete topics. It should establish an unmistakable separation between the topics, so that students are less likely to blur them or blend them. Avoid the book that follows the pattern common to many of the last generation and still evident in some today — a lead case, a note case, two rhetorical questions, a horizontal line, and on to the next topic.

8. Does the Book Have a Teacher's Manual — and, If So, Is It Any Good?

One factor to consider in selecting a book is whether it has a useful teacher's manual. This can be especially important if you are teaching the course for the first time and you are less than fully familiar with the subject matter. Due to the strange nature of law school casebooks — their pastiche of judicial opinions, statutes, law review fragments, and other miscellany, punctuated by abstruse musings and questions, with no real expository thread to bind it all together — any direct communication from the authors is welcome.

For law school casebooks, the teacher's manual is a relatively recent phenomenon. Twenty years ago they were quite rare, and they offered little more than a few supplemental cases or problems. We're not sure exactly how and when the teacher's manual as comprehensive guide caught on. But we do know that the Dukeminier[61] casebook was one of the first. Thanks in large part to its superb teacher's manual, Dukeminier has been very successful in the marketplace. One of us recalls a rueful tribute to that manual by a former colleague. This professor began his career at a very prestigious law school, but his teaching evaluations were less than sterling and he was now employed at a lesser (but still quite good) school. Looking back on his career, he once said: "If I had used Dukeminier, with that teacher's manual, I'd still be teaching at [his former school]."

How can you tell whether a teacher's manual is any good? A manual will be helpful if it explains *why* the authors put a particular case or statute or article into their book. What were they thinking? What were they trying to accomplish? When *they* are teaching out of this book, what points or questions or hypotheticals do they pursue when focusing on this particular passage? This information will be invaluable to you not only when preparing for each classroom session but even earlier, when you are deciding which passages in the book to include in your reading assignments. When determining whether a particular passage may be safely excluded from your syllabus, it will certainly be helpful to know why the authors put it there in the first place.

One indication of the usefulness of a teacher's manual is how well it addresses the comments and questions in the book. In an ideal world, you would have time to formulate your own answers to the author's questions and your own reflections on their comments. In the real world, your time is valuable and you may sometimes be scrambling to prepare for class — particularly your first time through the course. Beware, then, of any teacher's manual that fails to disclose how the authors themselves respond to the comments and questions in their book.

Another thing to look for is the depth of explanation in the manual. Even if you know the subject well and are not teaching it for the first time, the authors of the teacher's manual may offer perspectives or insights on a particular case that you haven't considered. Some manuals merely provide a case squib and a sentence or two; others go on and on with additional material. All other things being equal, more is better in judging a teacher's manual — and, all other things being equal, choosing the casebook with the better manual makes sense.

Nowadays some publishers will give you the teacher's manual in *electronic* form. Often this option is available, but only if you know to ask. This can certainly be very helpful, enabling you to incorporate passages from the manual directly into your lecture notes, but a word of caution is necessary. Avoid pouring long stretches of the manual straight into your notes. Try instead to be extremely selective in what you adopt from the manual. The danger here is that you'll incorporate so much material that you'll wind up covering points that are too obscure to warrant extended attention, rather than building your notes based on your own sense of priorities.

C. DESIGNING A SYLLABUS

Now that you've selected a casebook, you'll have to determine the length and sequence of your reading assignments, setting them forth in a syllabus. Those reading assignments are critically important because they reflect the content, structure, and pace of your course. Accordingly, we offer extensive advice on how to construct your reading assignments. After that, we provide suggestions on what else to include in your syllabus.

1. Constructing Your Reading Assignments

a. Don't Try to Cover Too Much Ground

Don't imagine that your students will digest the material with the same level of understanding regardless of how many pages of reading you assign each night. The more ground you attempt to cover, the more superficial will be their comprehension. When determining your reading assignments, your biggest challenge will be to strike a proper balance between achieving adequate coverage of the key topics in your course and giving your students a manageable number of pages each night to allow comprehension. It is important to realize that understanding will be lessened if you try to stretch the coverage too far.

If all you care about is coverage, then it's simple enough to march through the casebook, assigning every page. But that will probably require you to race through forty or fifty pages of text per every class hour. Covering the whole book may make it easy for you to determine the assignments (you won't have to do any editing), but it will take a toll on your students.[62] You should keep in mind that yours is not their only class. But even if you did have their undivided attention, covering forty or fifty pages per class hour is simply too hurried. To achieve a meaningful grasp of the material, law students need to travel at a much more gradual pace — giving them time not just to read it, but to absorb it.

Coverage is important — but it's meaningless if you are shoveling material at your students faster than they can digest it. You have no business congratulating yourself for covering the Statute of Frauds and the Parol Evidence Rule all in a single class session if your students are left unable to tell them apart. Coverage without comprehension really isn't coverage at all.

In our experience, student comprehension is impaired as you begin to travel faster than twelve to fifteen pages per class hour with first-year students and faster than twenty to twenty-five pages per class hour with upper-division students. Even at this pace (and even if you have only a limited number of goals), you will find it challenging to do a solid job of basic analysis, with time left over to blend in as much theory and/or practical overlay as you would desire. With the foregoing parameters in mind, we recommend that you err on the side of covering less rather than more material, traveling slower rather than faster, and searching for a balance that favors comprehension over coverage.[63]

b. Identifying the Topics to Be Included in Your Course: What to Cover When You Can't Cover Everything

As we've already observed,[64] most casebooks are *designed* to include more material than you can comfortably cover in a single course. So assigning the entire book is inappropriate. Instead, it's your job to *edit* the book, cutting it down to a manageable size. When making those cuts, what principles should guide your decision making?

First, you should identify the topics or doctrines that are so central to your course that they must be given priority in terms of coverage. These would include any topic that is traditionally associated with your course and that students would be expected to learn as part of the foundation of their legal education. In identifying such a topic, ask yourself whether students will be responsible for knowing it on the bar exam and whether yours is the only course in which students are likely to learn it. If the answer to both of those questions is "yes," the topic probably deserves to be covered.[65]

Next, go back and examine the specific goals that you have decided to pursue in teaching the course.[66] Ask yourself whether those goals directly implicate any of the topics that appear in your casebook's table of contents. If so, such a topic should be singled out for inclusion.

Next, if you are teaching a first-year course, ask yourself whether there is anything your students will need to learn from you in preparation for their upper-division courses. Any topics falling within this category would deserve inclusion as a second-tier priority.

At this point, you will have identified the core topics to be covered in your course. Yet to be determined is whether you'll have room for additional topics and, if so, how many. You simply won't know until you begin plotting out the reading assignments for your core topics and it becomes apparent how many pages they consume.[67]

If it turns out that you can comfortably include some additional topics, then you should perform a second review of your casebook's table of contents. At this point, you should rank the remaining topics at varying levels of priority. In doing so, you might use any of the following criteria: degree to which exposure to the topic is necessary for a meaningful grasp of your subject area; degree to which a given topic introduces concepts that you are committed to covering; likelihood of inclusion on the bar exam; relevance to current or future practice in your subject area; closeness of connection to one of your core topics; level of current scholarly, political, or commercial attention that the topic has generated.

Finally, when trying to distinguish the topics that you will cover from the topics that you won't cover, remember this: You don't have to cover every topic at the same level of detail. When crafting your reading assignments, there is nothing wrong with singling out one or two core topics for greater depth of coverage, while going into less detail on others. By doing so — by trimming the number of pages that your students have to read for some topics — you may be able to make room for a subject or an objective (such as skills training) that you might otherwise have been forced to exclude.[68] These "trims" are accomplished by assigning fewer than all of the pages that your casebook devotes to a given topic. When making such trims, we suggest that the priority should be to preserve those pages that set forth the basic concepts and the doctrinal rules, along with any cases that best exemplify those concepts and rules. Trims are best reserved for material that is duplicative, confusing, outdated, or illustrative of applications or exceptions with little relevance to current practice. Occasionally, a casebook will present three cases that all make the same basic point. You might want to cut two of those cases as needlessly duplicative. But read them carefully before doing so. If the cases feature differing outcomes — each of them turning on the presence or absence of certain pivotal facts — then there may be strong pedagogical reasons for keeping all three of them. Viewed in combination, the three cases may be an excellent vehicle for teaching your students legal analysis.[69] If you are having trouble with this type of editing, take a look at your teacher's manual. Some manuals will give you advice on how to edit *within* a topic if you are not planning to cover all of the pages that the author devoted to that topic.

Finally, when it comes to making these editing choices, don't expect to be exactly right about every decision the first time you teach a course. Inevitably, you'll revise some of them the next time through. If in retrospect you wish you had cut a topic or case that you originally included, don't get down on yourself; such fine-tuning is part of the game. To protect yourself the first time through, select or consult a casebook that follows a conventional progression of material, and inform your editing decisions by conferring with colleagues and examining outside sources like bar review outlines.

c. Ordering the Progression of Topics: Logical Isn't Necessarily Pedagogical

Now that you've identified the topics to be covered, you need to determine the *order* in which you'll cover them. When charting the progression of topics, remember that you need not follow the sequence employed by your casebook. Of course, you may have chosen that casebook precisely because you agreed with its organizational structure.[70] But don't let that dissuade you now from undertaking a fresh, independent look at how your topics should flow. The decisions that you make on this particular matter will have a huge impact on how your students experience your course.

What are the key questions to be asking yourself here? A very important question is whether there are any topics to which the students must first be exposed in order to understand certain other topics.[71] More generally, you should be asking yourself how the topics may be sequenced so as to give your students the best opportunity to understand the material. In many courses, this may involve dividing the topics into carefully segregated issues, elements, or steps. By means of this device, your syllabus can give students a big-picture perspective on how the topics fit together. So, for example, in teaching a Civil Procedure course, it might be preferable to cover the Rules not in numerical sequence but in the order in which they arise during the litigation of an actual case.[72]

Unfortunately, ordering your topics in a logical progression is not always pedagogically sound. It's often true that you can greatly enhance your students' understanding of the material by arraying the topics in the sequence that would seem logical to someone who is already familiar with the topic. But there are at least two situations where logical is not pedagogical.

First — and this is a point that does not only apply to first-year, first-semester students — you don't want to begin the semester with an exceedingly difficult, recondite, or abstract topic. This can leave a large number of students confused and demoralized at the very outset. It's better to begin the semester with a doctrinal overview of your subject, or to present an introductory hypothetical that foreshadows themes or doctrines central to your course.[73] Then, to give them a sense of confidence and to get them accustomed to your classroom methods, begin with material that is comparatively less difficult and less important. For example, if you're teaching Torts, it might occur to you that negligence is the most important and central topic, and therefore the right one with which to start the course. Once students have learned this material, you might think to yourself, you can breeze through intentional torts at the very end of the semester or year. But if you think about the perspective of a student in the first weeks of law school, it may be better to *begin* with intentional torts. In contrast to the murky waters of negligence, the law of intentional torts is comparatively easy to grasp. The elements are clearer and the material is more straightforward. Though it may not be the *logical* place to start, it's *pedagogically* advantageous for being less likely to overwhelm your students when they are first learning how to study, how to conduct themselves in class, and how to gauge your expectations. Another example of this comes from the Contracts course. Contracts professors debate endlessly whether to begin the course with damages or with offer and acceptance. Many sophisticated professors regard remedies as the key to the course — because there is little value to learning *whether* a contract has been breached if we are left in the dark about *what* the victim will receive. But damages is a recondite topic, far more daunting than the rules of offer and acceptance.[74] If we look at the problem once again from the perspective of a student who is new to law school, the *logical* starting point may not make the best *pedagogical* sense.

Second, you don't want to leave a key section of the course until the very end of the semester. We call this "saving the best for last," and it's a mistake that even seasoned professors make. Why do they do it? Often because the topic is situated at the very end of their casebook, or because they feel that the topic follows logically from and builds upon certain preceding materials. The danger of doing this is that you *may not reach* the final reading assignment in your syllabus. Thus, you'll come to the end of the semester without having covered a key section of your course. Or, in order to reach that final section, you'll hurry through the preceding sections and leave your students confused and dismayed. Either scenario should be avoided. Instead, structure your reading assignments so that there is no significant danger that you'll fail to reach any of your core topics. Do this even if it means departing from a logical progression of topics. Students are capable of understanding a topic encountered out of order, particularly if care is taken to explain where that topic fits in the larger scheme of your course. Then, develop a list of new topics or elaborations of earlier topics that can be introduced in the final week or two of the semester. It can actually be an advantage to come back to a topic for greater depth of coverage, or to explore a sub-topic that relates to material previously covered, as it provides a good vehicle for review. In this way, you can take the awkward problem of how to end the semester and turn it to your advantage by making it an opportunity for review.

Having said this, we do caution professors, particularly in the early years of their careers, that deviating too often from the order of the book tends to elicit a negative reaction from students. For reasons that aren't entirely clear, students seem to be suspicious of these re-orderings. We do believe that if you follow our advice about "transparency"[75] and "situating the material,"[76] and if you convey *why* you've made these adjustments, the students' apprehension can be reduced or eliminated.

d. Avoiding the "Marbury Gap"

By exhorting you to avoid the "Marbury Gap," here is what we mean: When charting the sequence of your reading assignments, try to avoid long passages that provide background rather than conventionally tested material. The classic example relates to the famous case of Marbury v. Madison,[77] which established the power of judicial review. It is typical of many Constitutional Law books to present the case and then follow it with extended textual material on the decision's validity and implications. While the importance of *Marbury* is undeniable, we doubt that many professors actually test their students on the legitimacy of judicial review. Logically, the issue of *Marbury*'s "correctness" comes up at this point in the course. But a careful examination of Marbury can easily consume two or three weeks of class time (and much longer when you consider the inevitable inclusion of Martin

v. Hunter's Lessee[78] and other seminal decisions of the Marshall Court). Well before those weeks are up, you will have lost your students if they cannot perceive any connection between *Marbury* and the contemporary issues of constitutional law on which they expect to be tested. Thus, a "Marbury Gap" is a long stretch of textual material, often theoretical or historical, that is so basic, or so remote, or so abstract as to be unlikely to be tested in a conventional manner, thus causing problems in the parceling out of assignments.

We are not saying that *Marbury* is unimportant; we are saying that it's not tested by most professors in the conventional manner. The idea of judicial review acts as a backdrop and an assumption of the course. But seldom would this foundational concept be featured on an issue-spotting, doctrinal exam question. You need to consider what the reading assignments during this portion of the course will look like, and what sort of class discussion you can expect to generate if the assignment for the day is simply textual reading. This same concern arises in other law school courses. In Criminal Law, for example, many casebooks devote a long section to theories of punishment. The importance of that material is undeniable — but it is often comprised of abstruse musings from the likes of Immanuel Kant. Once again, this is not the kind of material that lends itself to rule-based law school testing.

There is another aspect to this — and *Marbury* again serves as an example. In the pages following *Marbury*, most casebooks raise the question of whether or not judicial review is a good idea. But at this point in the course, your students probably haven't read a single substantive decision of the Supreme Court other than *Marbury* itself. Thus, your debate on judicial review takes place in a vacuum. Such material may be better handled by raising the broad question and themes, but returning to the particulars only later, once the students have more of the course under their belts.

How do you deal with a Marbury Gap? Consider breaking up the background or theoretical material into smaller pieces and turning it into a recurrent theme — one that you briefly introduce and later return to from time to time, tying it (if you can) to what your students are currently learning. Let's again look at *Marbury*. Use it initially to introduce the concept of judicial review. Come back to it later, especially when examining the separation of powers and the Supreme Court's role in construing individual liberties and the scope of federal legislative power. Viewed from those perspectives later in the semester, the legitimacy of judicial review and its crucial role in our system of checks and balances will have more meaning for your students. On those later occasions, you can assign the notes following *Marbury* to explore questions of theory or policy that your students would have been less able to appreciate at the semester's outset.

e. Waiting for the Right Time to Address Theory or Policy

The proper *sequencing* of the information you convey is critical to effective teaching:

> [T]he job is to figure out what to say and when and how to say it. First you have
> to get your audience's attention. Once you've done that, you have to present your

message in a clear, logical fashion — the beginning, then the middle, then the ending. You have to deliver the information the way people absorb it, a bit at a time, a layer at a time, and in the proper sequence.[79]

This quotation provides excellent advice for teachers, but it was never meant for the classroom — it was written to advise business owners on how to get their message across in a retail setting. As teachers, we should be just as interested as Nordstrom or Target in sequencing the information we convey so it can be readily absorbed. We must be sensitive to sequencing on both the micro level (ordering the progression of ideas when introducing a new topic or doctrine) and the macro level (ordering the progression of topics or doctrines over the span of a whole semester). When it comes to sequencing, be particularly careful about when to expose your students to theory or policy.

Students are much more receptive to discussions of theory or policy if they have first been exposed to some concrete examples of the *context* in which that theory or policy will play out. Thus, when charting the sequence of materials you will cover, our advice is this: Don't front-load theory or policy without first giving the students a real case to sink their teeth into. Particularly with any first-year course, you risk losing your students if you start out with abstractions. Let them see some facts and rules first. Then, after two weeks or so, go *back* over the same material and tease out the strands of theory and policy. Your students will be better equipped to grasp such material then.

For example, in Contracts you certainly want to expose your students to the theories and policies that govern the enforceability of promises. But if you commence your course with a lecture or discussion of enforceability in the abstract, you won't reach many students. By contrast, if you begin with offer-and-acceptance hypotheticals, varying the facts so that contract formation is achieved in some but fails in others, you are giving your students a tangible context in which to discuss enforceability. Now you can go back over those hypotheticals and get your students talking about whether and why formation is warranted. Through this exercise, you can get them to see the policy and theoretical underpinnings of the rules that govern contract formation.

In the realm of Constitutional Law, Professor Erwin Chemerinsky provides an excellent example of how to deal with matters of theory. His casebook explores the differing theories of constitutional interpretation not in the abstract but in a factual context that students can readily grasp: the "right to bear arms" under the Second Amendment.[80] Using this familiar clause and recent cases construing it, Chemerinsky is able to expose students to a variety of interpretive methods, including the use of original intent, historical tradition, the plain meaning of the text, and the impact of adjoining or modifying language. Presented in the abstract, these interpretive methods would not likely inspire much class discussion. But offered in the context of a hot-button political controversy, they are much more likely to generate a vigorous exploration in the classroom.

f. Don't Tie Yourself Down to Covering Particular Pages on Particular Dates

While charting your reading assignments, you must remain cognizant of how many class sessions comprise your semester and how many pages you can comfortably cover in each class. You should be keeping track of where you expect to be in your casebook by the end of each class session. It's important that you be aware of this, so that you don't fall too far behind.

But those calculations are for your eyes only.[81] Our advice: Do not put them in your syllabus. Do not tell your students that particular reading assignments are linked to particular dates. Why not? Because you don't want them focusing on whether or not you're "on schedule." Their sole focus should be on learning the material. You don't want them distracted by concerns that something is "wrong." This can cause them to draw all sorts of unsettling conclusions. They might assume, for example, that you are incompetent or that they are too stupid to keep pace. Protect them from overreacting in these ways by taking our advice.

There is another problem with assigning firm dates to particular reading assignments. It puts pressure on *you*, the professor, to speed up toward the end of class.[82] As you glance down and see that you are several pages away from "completing the day's assignment," you are more likely to accelerate, whether or not that pace is justified by the material and your students' comprehension. There is nothing wrong with leaving some of a day's assignment for the next class session. Simply begin the next class with a recap and then a segue to the remainder of the previous assignment.

The important thing to remember here is that you are a teacher, not a train conductor — and you need the flexibility to slow down or speed up based on how your students are responding to the material. It's important that you maintain an internal clock to stay apprised of your own ideal schedule. But it serves no beneficial purpose to hand that clock to your students. In the end, that clock is not nearly as important as whether they are gaining a good grasp of the material. Do your best to stay on schedule, but don't regard it as your top priority.

2. What Else Should Be Included in Your Syllabus?

Your reading assignments aren't the only item to be included in your syllabus. It's wise to include the administrative ground rules for your course along with any expectations you have for your students. In this way, your syllabus can protect you from being accused later in the semester of failing to communicate various rules and requirements for your course. If a student violates your attendance policy, for example, it will be very easy to show that the policy is set forth in your syllabus and that all students were given a copy of it on the first day of class. For this reason, it's smart not only to pass out your syllabus at the very outset of the semester but also to review it, page by page, with your students. Moreover, if you maintain a course Web page,[83] be sure to post a copy of your syllabus there.

What follows is a list of components that we recommend including in your syllabus.

A. Required and Recommended Texts
B. How You May Be Contacted; Scheduling of Student Appointments; Office Hours
C. How You Plan to Conduct Your Class
    1. Manner of Calling on Students
    2. Cases/Problems/Other
    3. Your Expectations as to Classroom Participation
    4. How You Will Field Questions
    5. How You Will Deal with Student Unpreparedness
D. Your Attendance Policy
E. Course Web Page, If Any
F. Course Listserv, If Any
G. How You Will Test and Grade Your Students
H. Policy on Audio Taping of Class Sessions
I. Policy on Use of Laptop Computers in the Classroom[84]
J. Review Session(s), If Any
K. Special Dates, If Any
L. Materials, If Any, on Reserve in the Law Library
M. Reading Assignments

IV. In the Classroom: Overarching Precepts

By now you've chosen a book, created a syllabus, and charted your objectives for the course. Soon you'll be stepping into the classroom. At this point, let's look at classroom teaching from a big-picture perspective.

A. PLAY THE ROLE

From the moment you enter the classroom, you must play the role of a law school professor. Students expect it — and you don't want to commence your relationship with them by violating their most basic expectations. What does it mean to "play the role"? It means that you conduct yourself in a professional manner, taking care not to be extremely informal or familiar with your students. It means that you show respect for your students and for the study of law. It means that you manifest a seriousness of purpose and a genuine commitment to helping your students learn. If you follow our advice, you'll be transparent[85] about your expectations — but this does not mean letting the students in on every internal debate you've had about every nuance of the course. Voicing continual self-doubt will not earn you credibility; it will undermine it. Ultimately, everything we say and do in the classroom serves as an example to our students of appropriate professional behavior. In a word, we must *model* professional behavior — it's our inescapable role.

B. FIND YOUR OWN VOICE

Within the parameters of playing the role, you have plenty of room for individuality. What will you be like in the classroom? Tough and demanding? Patient and sympathetic? Or perhaps a stance that mediates between those extremes? Whatever persona you choose, you must be able to sustain it. As a rule, then, you don't want to stray too far from your basic personality. But there is one important exception to that rule: In adopting a classroom persona, you should deviate from your basic personality to the extent required by the needs of your students. If you firmly believe that your students will not learn unless you are more than characteristically demanding of them, you should adjust your classroom persona accordingly. Likewise, you may see the need to display far more patience in the classroom than your personality would normally admit. This question — how to create a classroom atmosphere conducive to learning — goes to the very heart of your teaching philosophy. We address it below,[86] but it remains a deeply personal question that only you can answer. If humor is a natural part of your personality, you can use it now and then to ease your students' anxiety.[87] If you resolve to err on the side of toughness, there are a few points worth remembering. First, if you adopt a demanding attitude with your students, you need to temper it with a strong dose of realism. In other words, don't demand the impossible from them. Bear in mind that learning the law is a struggle even for intelligent people. Especially with first-year students, you should expect their progress to be tentative and halting. Second, it is better to start tough and gradually let up than vice versa. Finally, don't demand something of your students if you don't truly believe that it's necessary to their success.

C. DON'T BE "GENERIC" — INJECT SOMETHING OF YOURSELF INTO THE COURSE

Every law professor was shaped by the career path that brought her to academia, so each of us brings a unique package of skills and experiences into the classroom. Whether you clerked for a federal judge, or worked for the SEC, or handled mergers and acquisitions for a big firm, or tried First Amendment cases for the ACLU, you entered the teaching profession with special insights into certain areas of the law. Don't be shy about *using* those insights to enrich your teaching.

For example, let's say that you were a trial lawyer before entering academia. If you find yourself teaching Evidence or Civil Procedure, why not give your students some special exposure to the art of jury selection? This is a topic that is almost completely neglected in law school — but it's a critical part of trying a case. You could devote as little as five minutes to it, merely lecturing on strategy and mechanics, or you could turn it into a full-blown exercise, with students playing the roles of the trial attorneys and the prospective jurors. Either way, your students will be enriched by the expertise that you have brought from the courtroom to the classroom.

Let's take another example. Maybe you came to academia after doing transactional work for a big firm. If you find yourself teaching Contracts, why not give your students a drafting exercise? You could build into that exercise some of the insights and lessons that you learned during your big firm days. Since ambiguous clauses often lead to litigation, maybe you could tie the exercise to a contract interpretation case in your casebook. Finally, you could work with your students to discover clearer contract language so that litigation could be avoided. Through this exercise, your students will benefit in a variety of ways. They will get a vivid sense of how a real-world contract is worded. They will learn some valuable lessons about contract drafting. And they will see the connection (often obscure for students) between the use of ambiguous language by the contract drafters and the need for judicial interpretation of that language if the parties dispute its meaning.

D. BE TRANSPARENT

Be *transparent* with your students — be open in revealing the structure of your course, identifying key points to be retained from a given lesson, situating the topic you're covering in its larger doctrinal context, and flagging important transitions as you move through the semester. Come right out and *tell* them your goals for the course, the skills you want them to develop, even your pedagogical reasons for making particular demands upon them.

Why be transparent? Because law students are slow to perceive the fundamental differences between law school education and undergraduate education. They can see (without knowing why) that the teaching *methodology* is often starkly different in law school. But they fail to see that law professors have very different goals and expectations for their students. They fail to see that a law student must study much differently from her undergraduate counterpart. And they fail to see that the job of a law student is to master a very different set of skills. Some of them will labor for months under the misconception that law school is just a continuation of the undergraduate experience — and they will be stunned when they receive bad grades in law school for the type of performance that earned them praise in college. Other students, taking their cue from the novelty of the classroom experience in law school, will realize that something different is expected of them from law professors — but they won't know exactly what it is. For some, the daily dose of discussion centered around cases will lead them to the (usually) false conclusion that the cases are what's important on the exam. The more a professor does with the cases (for example, giving historical background and profiles of the litigants to make the cases come to life), the more this misconception will be fed.[88] For many students, the Socratic method — by "Socratic" we mean not merely the questioning of students but the classical method of classroom interrogation exemplified by Professor Kingsfield in *The Paper Chase*,[89] where the teacher *only* asks questions and provides no answers — the Socratic method will seem pointless, malicious, and opaque, a bow of submission to some antiquated tradition. It will strike them as an impediment to understanding, and it will leave them mystified about what they should have learned in a given class session.

The best way to clear up these problems is to be transparent with your students, disclosing your expectations, identifying the skills you want them to acquire, suggesting study methods and outlining approaches, and summarizing the key points you want them to draw from any particular lesson. Since the Socratic method can be baffling to students, we suggest that you introduce or conclude any Socratic interlude with a direct explication of your aims in performing it, both pedagogical and substantive. By doing this, you will help your students make a successful transition to law school — and you will enhance their ability to get the most out of your instruction.

An important aspect of being transparent is to situate any given topic you're covering in its larger doctrinal context. By "situating" the material, we mean to identify where it fits within the body of law covered by your course.[90] For example: "Today we'll be focusing on the *promise* element in the cause of action for promissory estoppel." Or: "We turn now to the doctrine of 'true threats.' This is a category of unprotected speech. It is one of five such categories, along with fighting words, obscenity, child pornography, and the advocacy of imminent lawless action." This "situating" technique is especially helpful to students at the beginning of a class session or when you first introduce a new topic or doctrine. Though it may seem to you that you're stating the obvious, most students have terrible difficulty seeing where any given lesson fits within the larger doctrinal scheme. All too easily, such students can fall into a frame of mind in which every new lesson merely resembles another tree in a vast forest of similar trees. By situating the material on a regular basis as you move through the semester, you help your students to gain a big-picture perspective on how the doctrinal components of your course fit together. Of all the benefits of transparency, this may be the most valuable.

It is also wise to be transparent about your homework assignments and other course management decisions. Students often find it helpful to be shown *why* you have given them a certain line of cases to read — because it reveals to them how those cases fit into the larger body of law they are learning, and thereby gives them a sense of what to look for when reading those cases. Transparency is beneficial even when it comes to purely administrative decisions that you must impose, like rescheduling a make-up session. The point is that if you show the students that you have given the matter careful thought and weighed the available options, they will be much more likely to give you some slack, even if they dislike the end result.

E. CREATE A CLASSROOM ATMOSPHERE CONDUCIVE TO LEARNING

No matter how carefully you plan — no matter how much attention you devote to your questions and hypotheticals and visual aids — you will fall short of reaching your students if you do not create a classroom atmosphere conducive to learning.[91] Unfortunately, there is no magic formula for concocting the right atmosphere. Achieving it is more art than science. But it all emanates from you. Much of it is determined by your demeanor — by the way you regard your students and by your attitude toward teaching. Do you approach teaching with a spirit of generosity, with abundant patience, and with empathy for your students — or do you convey and project weariness, cynicism, hostility, or condescension? Are you there to help your students — or do you sometimes humiliate, belittle, trap, or nitpick? Are you attracted to teaching primarily because it offers you extended opportunities to show off in front of people who are in no position to challenge you? Are you so demanding and intimidating that your students cannot think straight? Are you so bored with the subject, or so unsure of yourself, that you feel the need to make the material far more complicated than it really is? These attitudes are visible to your students — and they determine, more than any other factor, the atmosphere in your classroom. Your competence and preparedness are vital, of course, but nothing is more important than your attitude. And there is one particular attitude that goes the longest way toward creating the right atmosphere: the unmistakable sense that you *care* about helping your students learn. Your goal should be getting your students to see that it is not you against the class, but rather you and the class against the material.

F. ENGAGE YOUR AUDIENCE

As a classroom teacher, one of your prime strategic objectives is to inspire student participation and engagement. There is no single way to achieve this. We have each found success using very different techniques. So in this section we offer you a variety of choices — from the tactical use of the seating chart to "expert panels" to courtroom simulations.

1. Tactical Use of the Seating Chart

Ahhh, the seating chart! We all remember it ruefully, no matter how long ago we graduated from law school. But don't disdain the seating chart just because you didn't like it as a student. After all, it's only a chart — it doesn't *have* to be used sadistically. Placed in compassionate hands, it can be a gentle tool for coaxing even the shyest students out of their cocoons. Though seating charts are often associated with professors who leap from student to student, calling on them in rapid-fire succession, or with those who single out one unfortunate soul and bore in on him, the mere use of a seating chart does not compel any particular method of interrogation. What it *does* provide is a fluid *transition* from one student to the next, so that you won't fumble around while trying to identify each new student whom you address. Such fumbling can destroy your pacing when you're getting lots of hands and you need to make split-second decisions about whom to call on next. Fumbled names and awkward pauses can distract your students, derailing their train of thought and preventing them from grasping the point you're trying to make. With a seating chart, you won't lose your momentum every time you shift to a new student or decide among the hands — and this works especially well if you single out the student *first* and *then* ask the question. If you call the student's name *after* asking the question, you're much more likely to get a deer-in-the-headlights reaction. Those awkward silences can hurt the pacing and continuity of your presentation just as much as any fumbling with student identification.

How do you go about constructing a seating chart? Some law schools will provide you with a blank chart — a simple diagram of "seats" (squares) arrayed in a classroom formation. If your school can't give you a chart, you can easily draw one yourself. Once you have a blank diagram, you'll have to decide how to go about filling it with your students' names. You can give them assigned seats, perhaps arranging them in alphabetical order, but this may seem unduly regimented. Another option is that, on the first or second day of class, you can ask them to choose their seats and to write their names in the corresponding squares on your chart. If you're teaching a two-semester course, strongly consider asking them to choose new seats at the outset of the second semester. This can help to revitalize the conversational dynamic in your classroom. By mixing up their accustomed seating pattern, you can sometimes generate a greater contribution from students who were previously reticent. If you periodically break the class into small discussion groups, a new seating pattern will give your students a new set of neighbors — and this can give their discussions a freshened perspective.

Some schools will give you small pictures of all your students so that you can create a seating chart with matching names and faces. This is well worth the effort because, even if you employ a conventional seating chart, you will be slow to learn many of your students' names. You'll quickly become familiar with the students who sit directly in front of you — but those who are situated at the outskirts of your peripheral vision will long remain an undifferentiated mass. Any seating chart that juxtaposes the names and faces of your students is well worth studying at home early in the semester. It will accelerate your familiarity with those anonymous students who occupy the hazy edges of your classroom.[92]

If you want your chart to double as an attendance sheet, simply make multiple photocopies of it — one for every class session.[93] Place it near the front of the classroom each day and have your students sign it as they walk in. If you're willing to give them a few days each semester when they're allowed to be unprepared, you can have them communicate *that* fact as well when they sign in.

Another device to consider — whether instead of or in combination with your seating chart — is the use of name placards. Utterly commonplace in business schools, the name placard is a long cardboard rectangle bearing the student's name that sits on her desk immediately in front of her. The students simply bring them to class each day. One of us makes the presence or absence of placards on a given day a source of humor: "Do you think not having your placard means that I'm not going to call on you?" And there is always a standing offer that the professor will buy a drink at the fifth-year reunion for any student who still has their placard — since the placards will certainly become one of the students' most cherished mementos. That small piece of cardboard allows you to look simultaneously at the student and her name. With a seating chart, you have to locate the name and then locate the student, sometimes forgetting the name while *looking* for the student.[94] Think of the placard as an added layer of protection against fumbling your identification of students.

Now that we've gone to the trouble of making a seating chart, let's consider some of the possible advantages of using one. They can certainly be helpful whenever you're teaching a class with a large enrollment. To keep a large class engaged, many professors believe that it's necessary to call on a significant percentage of the students every time you meet. In a class of seventy or eighty students, that might entail calling on twenty people a day. To address twenty different students in a span of sixty or seventy-five minutes, you have to be moving at a very rapid pace, with no time for fumbled transitions. Even if you question whether it's really necessary to interrogate quite so many students (as we certainly do), the fluid transitions afforded by a seating chart are nevertheless desirable.

Another advantage of the seating chart is that it facilitates getting everyone involved, drawing out even those quiet students who will never raise their hands.[95] A seating chart can be used to ensure that the burdens of class participation are more evenly distributed. It can help to counteract the dominance of the "monopolizers," those insatiably eager students, always springing up like spawning salmon, who leave the vast majority of their classmates feeling deflated and listless.

Using the seating chart to draw out all of your students has the added advantage of giving you the most accurate reading of how the class is responding to your instruction. If you don't use the seating chart, if you're only hearing from volunteers, you won't get reliable feedback on how the class *as a whole* is digesting the material. Some professors — those, for example, who give multiple quizzes, or use clickers[96] or TWEN[97] — have certainly found alternative methods of getting feedback. But there is still great value in getting live verbal feedback day after day from a cross section of the class. Especially revealing is how a student *begins* giving an answer. It's often the very first thing she says that most clearly betrays whether she's lost or whether she understands the material. Such feedback will be all the more valuable if you probe the whole class roster — and that will be much easier to do with a seating chart.

2. Calling Upon Students at Random Versus the "Expert Panel" Approach

Whether or not you employ a seating chart, there are many different approaches to calling on students in the classroom. You could rely solely upon volunteers. But that will give many students a free pass, allowing them to maintain a semester-long silence and tempting them to neglect their homework. In the alternative, you could employ the machine gun approach, spraying questions all over the classroom in quick succession. This is a good way to hold their attention. But if you employ it too aggressively, it can become alarming and distracting to your students. You don't want the substance of your presentation to be upstaged by your technique. And you don't want to inspire so much anxiety in your students that the learning process is impaired. At the other end of the intimidation spectrum, you could employ the "expert panel" approach, in which students are notified days in advance that they will be called on to cover a specific case or a particular topic. This approach greatly reduces student anxiety. It gives you the luxury of calling on students who tend to be very well prepared. But for every student who is not a designated panelist, it is an invitation to slack off. Thus, each approach to calling on students involves a trade-off, affording you distinct advantages but saddling you with certain drawbacks. Random interrogation is a brusque way of forcing your students to do their homework. By threatening them with public embarrassment each day, it forces them to prepare exhaustively each night. But it can produce a classroom atmosphere in which many students are too anxious to think straight. Rather than focusing on what you're trying to teach them, they'll be preoccupied with a much more compelling drama: Who will be thrown into the spotlight next? The expert panel approach does away with this distraction. It gives non-panelists a better chance to learn by allowing them to relax, to follow the thread of your presentation, and to ask questions. And it gives every panelist a chance to shine, because advance notice ensures a high level of preparedness. This, in turn, helps you — because it's much easier to cover the material when every student you call on is well prepared. But it leaves you with a nagging question: Are your expert panelists the *only* students who bothered to prepare?

So it must be admitted that random interrogation and the expert panel approach both have built-in drawbacks — but those drawbacks can be mitigated. All that's necessary is to pursue each method in a less extreme form. Random interrogation can be made less threatening (and therefore less distracting) by jumping from student to student with less frequency and ruthlessness. It also helps if you follow a pattern that has some elements of predictability, so that students are not left constantly guessing about whom you'll call upon next. You might, for example, trace a deliberate path up and down the rows of your seating chart, or circle your classroom in clockwise fashion, proceeding day by day from one quadrant to the next. Admittedly, this is a retreat from complete randomness — but it helps to ease the levels of student anxiety and distraction that are produced by complete randomness. Likewise, the main drawback of the expert panel approach can be mitigated by employing that approach in a less extreme form. A student's temptation to slack off every day that he is not an expert panelist can be combated by increasing the number of students who are "on" each day. Rather than identifying only four or five expert panelists for each class session, you could divide the class in half, or in thirds, or in fourths, and then begin a rotation in which these groups take turns being the sole focus of your questioning.

The pedagogical advantage of random interrogation is that it better promotes active learning in your students. Here is how one of us explains it in his syllabus: "It is very easy to sit back, listen to someone else talk (whether professor or fellow student), and think that you understand what was said or could have given the same good answer. But without active participation, you may find that you have fooled yourself. Unless you are ready to participate in classroom discussion, and actually DO participate, you will not be getting that valuable feedback, nor will you be getting practice in applying what you are learning." There are many ways to encourage active learning[98] — including how you pose your classroom questions and where you begin the discussion — but requiring participation by randomly calling on students is a valuable tool. Of course its effect depends partly on how large the class is and how many students a professor normally calls on in a given session. Some professors may feel that the paternalism of forcing students to participate is unnecessary (because they are already motivated and engaged) or inappropriate (either because "they are adults" or because "it's up to them"). But in light of its capacity to promote active learning, a professor should not lightly forgo the use of random interrogation, especially when teaching first-year students.

If random interrogation is the method you choose, then you *will* encounter unprepared students,[99] and you'll need to have a fully developed strategy for dealing with them. One of us, while teaching at George Washington University, had a colleague (himself an experienced and excellent teacher) who ruefully stressed this point. "If you're teaching in the evening," he said, "they're not all going to be prepared. Even at a good law school, evening students — and some *day* students — won't be ready. You need to figure out in advance how you're going to handle this. You can either fight the battle every evening to force them all to be prepared or you can modify your approach, being rigorous without being overbearing, and draw upon the strengths that evening students bring with them to school." One approach, as we mentioned above,[100] is to give your students a specified number of class sessions each semester in which they're *allowed* to be unprepared. This policy, which should be set forth in your syllabus,[101] can include a proviso that any additional unpreparedness will be factored into the student's final grade. How else might you deal with unpreparedness? One option is to require the unprepared student either to answer your question or solicit help from a classmate. (We introduce this option by inquiring of the student, "Do you need to retain outside counsel?") This approach, even when employed with some levity or lightness of touch, forcefully reminds the student that his unpreparedness creates an extra burden for his classmates. This realization will hit him more vividly if *he*, rather than you, must choose his rescuer. Another way of dealing with the unprepared student is to reformulate your question so that it is no longer tied to the specific facts and context of the passage he did not read. In this way, you block him from bowing out — and you force him to think on his feet.

When you encounter unpreparedness, you should not overreact to it. Obviously, you don't want to send a signal that it's *OK* to be unprepared. But rookie teachers tend to take *personally* any failure of their students to live up to expectations — and this can make you all too likely to explode when confronted with persistent unpreparedness. What do these explosions look like? The classic example is the young teacher who slams his book down and storms out of the classroom. Our advice on this is very simple. Don't do it. You'll never live it down. Don't berate your students. Don't scream at them. Don't insult them. You may permanently destroy your ability to reach them — and you will make yourself ridiculous. There are plenty of other mistakes that you can make with relative impunity: packing too much into your syllabus, racing too quickly through your casebook, giving a final exam that's too hard. None of *those* mistakes will ruin your credibility. But exploding like Mount Vesuvius will do it.[102]

3. Other Ways to Encourage Preparation and Participation

One way to get your students more engaged is to break the class into small groups and set them to work on a short analytical exercise of your own design or from another source. If you make the groups small enough (two or three persons per group), then every student will be forced to play an active role.[103] The exercise would present your students with a fact pattern and ask them to determine whether the facts give rise to a cause of action. The ideal time to do this is right after you have finished covering an important topic. Let's say, for example, that you are teaching Contracts and you have just completed the materials on promissory estoppel. You can employ the exercise as both a culminating review of promissory estoppel and as an opportunity to hone your students' analytical skills. You might give your students twenty or thirty minutes to analyze the problem while you roam the classroom, listening in on their discussions. While doing so, you might intervene from time to time, encouraging your students to identify the separate elements of promissory estoppel and to single out the pivotal facts on which each element will hinge. When the discussion time limit expires, you can debrief each of the groups, getting them to tell the whole class how they analyzed the problem. Many students are energized by this type of classroom experience and find it a very helpful method of learning the material.[104]

Shorter conversations among small groups of students, where they might be asked to explain to one another their understanding of a case or doctrine, can also be effective. Such small group work addresses one concern often expressed about the law school experience — that it tends to encourage individual effort rather than teamwork. Small group exercises have the beneficial side effects of modeling cooperative behavior and helping students get to know each other. Small group participation may be particularly valuable to your students if their first-year or upper-level required courses are taught in large sections.

One way to spur your students to a higher level of preparation is to deviate from the conventional "entry question" when you begin the discussion of a new case. If the students can count upon you, time after time, to kick things off in the conventional manner — by asking the first student to "state the case" — they will have little incentive to push themselves beyond a superficial familiarity with the readings. With minimal preparation, most students can bluff their way through a statement of the case by quickly scanning the opening paragraphs of the opinion. This buys time for other students to take a fleeting look themselves and then, as the discussion unfolds, they can pick up the flow of it. Many law school graduates (perhaps some of the professors who are reading this article) employed this "go with the flow" method of classroom participation — but you shouldn't want *your* students to do it, and you don't want to be the *cause* of their doing it. The best way to fight this problem is to change your "entry question," shifting its focus from preliminary matters (facts/ procedural posture) to the heart of the case: "What is the *issue*?" By kicking things off in this way, you force the first student (and thus the whole class) to prepare more fully — to enter your classroom having already processed the legal question posed by the case and the court's holding in response to it. By *starting* the discussion at the heart of the case, you foreclose a favored tactic of the superficially prepared — those students who try to get easy class participation points by preemptively answering initial questions about the facts and procedural posture. By dispensing with those questions, you force everyone to engage the readings at a higher level. We take a closer look at "entry questions" later in this article, in the section that deals with "Scripting Discussion Flow."[105]

Another way to engage your students is to stage courtroom simulations in which they play the role of a trial attorney.[106] This technique is especially suitable for courses like Civil Procedure and Evidence.

In Civil Procedure, for example, your coverage of personal jurisdiction can culminate in oral arguments on a Rule 12(b)(2) motion to dismiss.[107] You can play the role of the judge. Your students can be paired off — with half of them arguing for, and half of them arguing against, dismissal. This works best if you supply the students with a limited number of cases (between six and ten) and you make it clear that your questions and their arguments must be confined to those cases. Don't force them to argue too long; five minutes is a good time limit. If you can create a fact pattern that presents a close call on the jurisdictional issue, such that both sides have roughly an equal opportunity to win, there is a very good chance that your students will have an enjoyable experience. Many of them will find it stimulating, and some will regard it as the highlight of their semester. In the process, their understanding of personal jurisdiction will take a quantum leap. Their analytical skills, and their confidence, will benefit as well.

In Evidence, courtroom simulations have the salutary effect of making the rules come to life. They are best introduced as short direct-examination exercises, in which the student plays the role of the directing attorney and you play the role of the witness. In each exercise, give the student a narrow, simple objective — laying the foundation for getting a contract admitted into evidence, or authenticating a gun, or invoking a hearsay exception. Once the students have mastered these exercises, you can advance to something more complicated — like qualifying an expert witness, or satisfying the requirements of present recollection refreshed.[108] Eventually you can introduce greater complexity, enlisting classmates to interrupt the direct examination with objections and assigning a student/judge to rule on those objections. By giving students this type of "hands-on" experience, you can stimulate them to a much higher level of engagement. In the process, you can overcome the greatest challenge faced by Evidence teachers — getting students to see the rules as tools rather than abstractions.[109]

G. READ YOUR AUDIENCE

During your first year of teaching, you will be so preoccupied with performing your basic duties in the classroom that you may barely perceive how your students are reacting. Are they confused? Are they getting it? Are they bored? Are they panicking? You won't know. You'll be so absorbed with your own responsibilities that you'll hardly notice the demeanor of your students. At best, you'll register some fragmentary perceptions. But gradually, as you gain more classroom experience, your students will come into clearer focus. After teaching for a few years, you'll be amazed by how much you can discern in your students' faces. This ability — to *read* the feelings and reactions of your students — can assist you in fine-tuning your presentation.

Reading your audience can help you to adjust your *pacing*, slowing down or speeding up in reaction to the level of understanding that your students display. Likewise, it can help you to adjust the *depth* of your coverage — probing the finer points with a class that devours the material and wants a challenge, or going back to basics with a class that is hyperventilating. If your classroom is filled with furrowed brows, you'll want to stop and revisit the topic that is troubling them. You might even create some new hypotheticals, giving them a fresh lens through which to view the material.

Obviously, you don't want to overreact to one or two students whose facial expressions or body language are particularly dramatic. You don't want to adjust the pacing or depth of your coverage unless you discern the same reaction in a significant number of students.[110] But every class will experience your course in a different way. Some will sail; others will stagger. By reading your audience, you are simply being watchful for those inevitable differences.

Taking the pulse of your audience can be accomplished more directly, of course, by asking for a show of hands. This can be especially helpful when you are trying to gauge their grasp of a new concept. For example, let's say that you're using a hypothetical to introduce the elements of fraud, and you're focusing specifically on the requirement of *scienter*. After laying out the facts in your hypothetical, you might ask for a show of hands in the following way: "How many people think that the defendant will not be liable unless he *intended* to deceive the plaintiff? How many people think that intent to deceive is unnecessary?" (At this point, you might ask a third question: "How many people are unable to raise their arms?") Through this simple device, you get immediate feedback on your students' comprehension. If you want your students to register their votes without being able to see how their classmates are voting, you can poll them electronically using TWEN[111] or clickers.[112]

H. IDENTIFY ONE OR MORE THEMES THAT YOU WILL WEAVE THROUGH THE COURSE

To help the students gain a big-picture grasp of your subject, try to identify one or more themes that loom large in your course. If you can find such a theme, be sure to broach it early in the semester. Then, as the weeks go by, invoke it now and then, using it each time to make sense of a given case or argument.

When teaching Contracts, for example, one of us concludes the first day of class by introducing a "recurrent theme" that runs through the case law and often explains the behavior of judges. It is the tension between doing justice under the unique facts of a particular case and trying to remain faithful to a set of clear, well-established rules.[113] As the course proceeds, he invokes that theme to make sense of some difficult cases — such as *Webb v. McGowin*,[114] where the absence of a bargained-for exchange did not prevent the court from finding consideration to enforce a promise. One way to view *Webb* is that the court was so intent upon reaching a just result that it "found" consideration where none existed. When a first-year student reads a case such as *Webb*, she comes away convinced that she'll never understand consideration. She doesn't initially see that, in a system based on precedent, a judge must pay lip service to established rules even while straining to get around them. This is the kind of situation where a big-picture theme can help students to see beyond the narrow holding of a case.

For teaching purposes, the best "recurrent themes" are those that reveal connections between different parts of your course, that offer insights into our legal system, or that identify the policies underlying a body of law.

I. THE BOTTOM LINE: TEACHING LEGAL ANALYSIS

As the first day of class draws closer, you will have so much on your mind that you can easily lose sight of your most important obligation — to teach your students how to perform legal analysis. You will have targeted a number of strategic goals, of course, but your students' most pressing need is to graduate from law school with a highly developed talent for legal analysis. This is the skill that will sustain their careers. It will guide them even when faced with issues that you could never have foreseen. It will aid them even when the substantive law that you've taught them has been superseded. The responsibility for teaching legal analysis falls to you — and to every other teacher at your school. It is not the special province of the legal writing instructors. It is not uniquely the burden of the first-year professors. Only by practicing it again and again, in all of their classes, will your students be able to master it.

V. In the Classroom: The First Day

A. SETTING THE TONE

The moment you've been waiting for has finally arrived. You are standing before your students on the first day of class. How do you set the proper tone?

1. Let Them Know You Care

If your students see that you really *care* about helping them to learn and grow, then you will have traveled a long way toward creating the right atmosphere.[115] How do you show them that you care? There are no magic words for conveying it. But if you really *do* care, they will sense it right away. You can make it more apparent by talking to them about how you have designed the course. If they see that you are making every effort to be accessible to them; if they see that your teaching methods are designed to discipline their minds and to aid their understanding of the material; if they see that your approach to testing reflects a rigorous effort to be fair — then it will be obvious to them that you *do* care, very much, about their success. George Burns once said, "The secret of acting is sincerity. If you can fake that, you've got it made."[116] That may or may not be true of acting, but it won't work for teaching.

2. Establish Your Expectations

Now is the time — on the very first day of class — to establish your expectations. What do you expect of your students in terms of classroom preparedness and participation? What kinds of questions will you ask in class and what will you be looking for in the students' responses? What sorts of skills do you want your students to develop over the span of the semester?

In establishing your expectations, you should tell your students how they will be tested and what you will be looking for in grading their exams. It isn't necessary at this point to go into great detail. You can promise to do so later in the semester. What your students need now is to get a sense of the big picture. To paint that picture, one of us invokes his "unified field theory" of legal analysis — a term he shares with colleagues but not with students. Here is how he explains it to his class. There is no "trick" to exam writing apart from legal analysis itself. All legal problems are, at their core, a question of applying new facts to rules. This is true of what we do in the classroom, of what must be done on my exam, of what you'll need to do on the bar exam, and of what you'll have to do in practice. The facts will come to us in varying levels of detail and uncertainty, the rules in different degrees of clarity and "settledness," but in the end legal analysis is always the same enterprise — in the classroom, the law office, and the courtroom. For any given topic, the legal system has articulated what rules govern and therefore what facts are relevant. In a given situation, those rules are either satisfied or not, and the facts dictate that conclusion. In class, we may spend quite a bit of time discerning what those rules are (by case analysis or statutory interpretation), and then discussing whether, as a matter of policy or theory, those rules make sense. At other times, we may take the rules as a given, and see if particularly difficult facts fit the rules or not. In practice, there may be some cases at the cutting edge where the rules are up for grabs. In other cases the rules will be well settled. In some situations the facts will be neatly arrayed (as the facts tend to be on traditional law school exams) — but in many instances they won't be, and the lawyer's job will be to sift through the evidence and make sense of a client's convoluted story.

For students, the message here is that what you are training them to do in the classroom relates to what you want them to do on your exam, which relates to what they'll need to do when serving their future clients.*

B. SUGGESTIONS FOR STARTING THINGS OFF

On the first day, you'll need to take care of some basic housekeeping matters — passing around the seating chart,[117] going over the syllabus, and reviewing the administrative ground rules for your course. But we hope you won't settle for that. We think it's important to "do some law school" on the first day — to reach the *substance* of your course, preferably through interaction with your students. This can be done simply by covering the first case in your casebook, but there are some other approaches that we have tried over the years. Three of them are described in the subsections that follow. One of them, the Goodyear Blimp Overview,[118] is *not* interactive. It is essentially an extended lecture, taking students on a doctrinal "fly-over" of the black-letter law at the heart of the course. Students often find it tremendously helpful,[119] so we include it here even though it does not feature the student-teacher interaction that we recommend for the first day of class. (We normally employ it on the *second* day, after finding a way to engage our students on the first.) Student-teacher interaction *is* a key part of the *tabula rasa*[120] and foreshadowing[121] exercises described immediately below.

1. The Introductory Problem That Foreshadows Themes or Doctrines Central to Your Course

One way to get things started is to present your students with a fact pattern that is embedded with themes or doctrines that you will be exploring throughout your course. By sampling their reactions to the fact pattern,[122] you will often find in their viewpoints the gist of one of those embedded themes or doctrines. When this happens, you can immediately draw the connection between the student's observation and the theme or doctrine that they'll be learning about. Each time one of those embedded items is uncovered, you should write it on the board. At the end, simply by reviewing that list of items, you can present a preview of your course. This kind

---

* Some of your students don't need to be "sold," but for others, connecting the classroom to the "real world" of practice may enhance both motivation and understanding.

of foreshadowing will resonate with the students because their own observations were the centerpiece of the exercise.

Let's take, for example, the method by which one of us begins his First Amendment course. He uses a fact pattern that is based on a real case — one that he litigated,[123] settled,[124] and later wrote about.[125] He does not tell his students of his connection to the case because he does not want to inhibit their reaction to it. He uses this fact pattern because it is loaded with themes and doctrines that are central to the First Amendment course. Here, set forth verbatim, is the fact pattern that he gives to his students:

> This civil action, brought by inmates on Ohio's Death Row, is a First Amendment challenge to an Ohio prison policy that bars the condemned from uttering their last words in the moments before they are executed. Under this policy, the traditional privilege to make a last dying speech is replaced with a substitute — the opportunity merely to write out a "final" statement six hours before the execution. The challenged policy affords condemned prisoners no opportunity to make a last oral statement, audible to spectators, after being led into the death chamber for their final minutes of life. Under the policy, the prisoner is permitted merely to write out a final statement — to be distributed only after the prisoner is dead. In Count One of their complaint, the plaintiffs assert that this aspect of the policy violates the First Amendment. Plaintiffs allege that the policy is unconstitutional in a second respect. According to statements by Ohio prison officials when the policy was first adopted, the warden enjoys complete editorial control over the prisoner's statement, with unfettered discretion to change it, cut it, summarize it, or censor it altogether. The policy's aim is to prevent spontaneous and potentially unpleasant utterances by condemned prisoners as they await lethal injection. The Ohio Department of Rehabilitation and Correction has confirmed that the policy was adopted in response to dying speeches in other states, and is designed to shield the friends and relatives of murder victims from "potentially spiteful, profane, or abusive remarks" by those condemned to die. Plaintiffs seek declaratory and injunctive relief barring Ohio prison officials from enforcing the policy, and requiring them to restore to condemned prisoners the traditional opportunity to deliver a last dying speech in the moments before their execution.

After laying these facts before the students, he solicits their reactions. Since they have not yet learned any First Amendment law, he encourages them to offer up their "gut" responses. Often, one of their first observations is that prisoners probably do not or should not have the same speech rights as other citizens. This evokes a line of precedent that is covered in the course — the "restricted environment" cases, which recognize only limited speech rights in schools, prisons, and the military.[126] With each new reaction from the students, there is often a ready connection to another branch of First Amendment law. The doctrine of prior restraint[127] may be invoked when students express concern that the prisoner's written statement must be reviewed and approved in advance by the warden. The overbreadth[128] doctrine may be invoked when students observe that all dying speeches, even those expressing remorse and apology, are restricted under the policy. Lying at the very heart of this scenario — in the substitution of a censored written statement for an uncensored oral utterance, replacing the traditional death chamber speech with a writing produced six hours beforehand — is the critical difference between content-based restrictions and time/place/manner regulations.[129] Finally, the use of historical tradition in construing the Speech Clause may be invoked when students observe that dying speeches are a longstanding custom, perhaps centuries old.[130]

It must be admitted that this technique for kicking off a class can be risky to employ. But if you can find a fact pattern that is interesting enough to generate some class discussion, and if that fact pattern is embedded with enough themes or doctrines that are central to your course, then you will have the ingredients for a memorable start. By using their observations to foreshadow key elements of your course, you will simultaneously engage them and prepare them for a better understanding of your subject.[131]

2. Tabula Rasa: An Exercise in Creating the Law "from Scratch"

How can we prevent our students from passively accepting the law as they find it? How can we get them to confront the law's complexity with patience, not exasperation? How can we get them to look at the law from a fresh and critical perspective, viewing it in terms of what should be or might have been? These are among the greatest challenges that law professors face. Students tend to fall into passive acceptance when their only homework is reading appellate opinions. The whole enterprise breeds an uncritical acceptance of current precedent, an impatience with complexity, and an indifference to alternative paths that the law might have taken. We have found that students can be jarred out of this inertia by getting them to act as *creators*, rather than receptors, of the law. Asked to create a rule or doctrine "from scratch," *before* being exposed to current law on the subject, students tend to be open-minded, attuned to the need for nuance and complexity, and genuinely understanding of the difficulties faced by any rulemaker. Perhaps most important, they are forced to recognize that any rule has an underlying purpose and that it must be carefully tailored to achieve that purpose without causing unintended mischief. After trying their own hand at creating a rule, the students are very interested to see how their "law" differs from existing law. When performing this comparison, they approach the material with a level of attention and discrimination not normally attained in a conventional reading assignment. The students are much more cognizant of the fit between the rule's purpose and effect. They are in a much better position to appreciate any resort to nuance or complexity. They are better equipped to assess the rule critically. But they are also more likely to recognize the difficulties of creating the rule in the first place. In short, getting students to approach the law from a *rulemaker's* perspective prompts them to digest the material at a deeper level.

One of us has had particular success using this technique at the start of his Contracts course, in an exercise that focuses on the doctrine of consideration. The exercise confronts students with two questions: (1) In creating a law of contracts, are you going to make *every* promise enforceable? (2) If not, how will you distinguish between those promises that *are* enforceable and those that *aren't*? Students quickly realize that no legal system can make *every* promise enforceable, so they find themselves confronted with the very problem that consideration is meant to resolve. After they have struggled for a while to identify a basis for distinguishing between those promises that should and shouldn't be enforceable, they are genuinely interested to learn about the efforts of Oliver Wendell Holmes, Jr. to solve the same problem.[132] Even if they regard the Holmesian formulation — requiring a bargained-for exchange[133] — as somehow flawed, they are sympathetic to the difficulty of the task.

A number of benefits flow from this exercise. First, students come away with a vivid understanding of the *purpose* of the consideration doctrine, something that many law school graduates never comprehend. This is why so many law students moan and complain about the consideration doctrine. Since they don't have a clear picture of its purpose, they regard its extended treatment in the Contracts course as a cruel hoax by their professor. Second, after trying to create their own version of it, they are in a much better position to appreciate its halting development in the case law.

From a big-picture perspective, focusing a *tabula rasa* exercise on the doctrine of consideration is helpful to students in two respects. First, it reinforces the notion (often lost on students) that the Contracts course is all about the enforceability of promises. Second, it helps to make the consideration doctrine approachable and understandable to students — thereby alleviating one of the greatest obstacles in the course.

The *tabula rasa* method may be readily adapted to any law school course. It is best used in connection with any rule, doctrine, or concept that is fundamental to the course, especially if students have trouble getting a clear picture of its underlying purpose.

3. The Goodyear Blimp Overview: Taking Students on a Doctrinal "Fly-Over" Before Covering the Same Ground on Foot

Students find it very helpful to survey the broad outlines of a course from an "aerial" perspective before commencing a detailed study. We call this a Goodyear Blimp Overview, and it is meant to accomplish three objectives. First, it lays before your students the full range of topics that you will be covering — not necessarily in the same sequence that you will follow, but organized in a manner that best conveys their interrelation. Second, the overview provides a doctrinal introduction to each topic, laying out some of the basic black-letter law in each area.[134] Third, the overview touches briefly on the purpose or function of each topic. The overview is presented in a lecture format and typically consumes an entire class session.

If you are teaching a first-year subject, the students will find it particularly helpful if your overview lecture is accompanied by a one-page chart that displays all of the topics to be covered in your course, arrayed in a format that shows how they fit together. If you go to the trouble of creating such a chart, you can refer to it each time your overview lecture shifts to a new topic — and, as the semester progresses, you can refer back to it whenever you make a transition from one topic to another. In combination with such a chart, the Goodyear Blimp Overview inspires the gratitude of many students by helping them to maintain a big-picture perspective of the topics that comprise your course.[135]

VI. In the Classroom: Day-to-Day Teaching Techniques

A. WHY IT IS UNREALISTIC TO EXPECT STUDENTS TO LEARN EVERYTHING BY INDUCTION

The classical method of law school teaching — best exemplified by Professor Kingsfield in *The Paper Chase*[136] — restricted the instructor's role to that of a Socratic interrogator who, asking questions but never deigning to explain, prodded the students toward a tentative grasp of the cases in their casebook. Students were expected to learn the law not from any expository lecture (no professor worth his salt would stoop to such "spoon-feeding"), but by drawing inferences from the particular facts and holdings in the cases.* In short, the classical method of law school teaching discouraged direct communication between teacher and students, and forced students to do most of their learning through a process of induction.

This method of instruction wrapped the teacher in a pedagogical straitjacket, hampering her ability to assist the learning process. Inevitably, students were forced to rely on outside materials (hornbooks, commercial outlines, and other sources of direct exposition) to teach themselves what they could not learn solely through induction. And let's be honest: *You* didn't learn everything you know about the law by means of induction; *you* relied on treatises, law review articles, and perhaps even commercial outlines. So why should you expect your students to learn solely by reading appellate decisions and deciphering Socratic colloquies? Even if, as a student, you did rely only on induction (which, quite frankly, we doubt), is it fair to compare yourself with your students? Obviously, you were an exceptional student and became a professor. How many of them fall into that category?

It isn't "spoon feeding" to recognize that there are limits to learning by induction and that we do not weaken our students by resorting to direct methods of communication. Our exhortation to "be transparent"[137] is a plea to be open with your students not only about the structure and goals of your course but also its substantive content. To be sure, the Socratic method[138] can be very useful in training your students to extract doctrinal rules and analytical techniques from appellate opinions. But when a period of Socratic questioning comes to an end, can we safely assume that every student has absorbed every point that you were trying to convey?

---

* Apparently the theory is that if a student stares long enough at her casebook she'll come to understand not only the rule of the case but the limitations on that rule, the weaknesses of the judge's rationale, and the subtle connections among the cases.

Hardly. The Socratic method is too oblique, too reliant on suggestion, too dependent on induction ever to permit that assumption. Under the classical method of law school teaching, your job is done — you've gone as far as you can go in conveying those points. But if those points were worth communicating in the first place, why would you stop there? Why wouldn't you pause, even briefly, to sum up, or to draw attention to some of the more important points? There is no guarantee, of course, that your recapitulation will cause every student to grasp every point, but the likelihood of successful communication is better with it than without it. This is why we believe that any strict Socratic interlude should be followed by a direct summation of the key points that the professor was trying to convey.

B. SCRIPTING DISCUSSION FLOW

When planning your classroom coverage of any given case, you will have to decide how best to begin the discussion — you will have to find the right "entry question."[139] Your choice is important because the starting point of a discussion can affect its direction and depth. There are many different points where you might begin. You could ask the first student to recite the facts or state the case. You could ask for the issue or the governing rule. You could start at the end and work back, inquiring why or whether the plaintiff deserved to win. Each of those starting points could be defended as a legitimate choice. But some starting points will be better than others in generating a discussion flow that can be channeled in the direction you want — a discussion flow that travels through the topics you want to cover.[140]

When selecting an entry question, always begin by asking yourself: What are my objectives in covering this case? What lessons do I want my students to learn from it? Once you have formed a clear picture of those goals, ask yourself how they might be accomplished through class discussion — taking into account any difficulties in the opinion that might confuse or derail the discussion.[141] Then, using various entry questions, think through how the discussion might flow. If your entry question can lead to a dead end, or leave you stalled in a procedural quagmire, or deflect the discussion away from the central issue in the case, then you'll want to try a different entry question or prepare a response that will channel the discussion back toward your goals.

We believe that one particular goal is worth pursuing with virtually every case you cover — namely, training your students how to perform legal analysis. As explained more fully below,[142] we believe that students must be repeatedly prompted to identify the governing rule, to reduce that rule to elements, and to determine whether those elements are satisfied by the available facts. Thus, when orchestrating the discussion flow of any particular case, one of our principal aims is to steer the students through an element-by-element analysis of the plaintiff's claims. What sort of entry question paves the way to that analysis? An entry question that asks for the *issue* in the case, since asking for the issue is no different than asking for the governing rule. We have already suggested, at an earlier point in this article,[143] that students can be spurred to a higher level of preparation if your entry question regularly asks for the issue, rather than requesting a statement of the case or the facts. But beginning with the issue is beneficial for other reasons. It helps to avoid the dreary spectacle so often produced when the professor begins with: "Please state the case." What usually ensues is a long, laborious recitation of the facts — *all* the facts, relevant and irrelevant alike, delivered in a barely audible monotone. By starting with the issue, you force the students to zero in on the governing rule and to recognize that facts are relevant only insofar as they speak to the rule's requirements.

We are not suggesting that your entry question must always ask for the issue; in fact, there are many stimulating ways to launch a discussion,[144] and mixing in a little variety will keep your students on their toes. The important thing to remember here is that a carefully chosen entry question can help you steer the flow of discussion toward the lessons you want to convey. Moreover, it can reinforce the conception of legal analysis that you are trying to convey — applying new facts to what the legal system considers to be relevant.

C. "STAY BACK, THEN QUICK"[145]

This quotation comes from the world of baseball, but it can be fruitfully applied to classroom teaching. In its original context, it was meant to describe the essence of hitting: Keep your hands and your weight back until the very last instant so that you can accurately read the speed and the spin of the approaching ball; don't lunge at it prematurely. Translated from the realm of baseball to teaching, this exhortation means that we shouldn't be hasty to cut off student discussion. Instead, we should lay back and allow them as much time as possible to think through the question at hand — giving them every opportunity to discover (and therefore "own") the correct answer. Only at the last moment should we jump in to clarify the point.

This advice recognizes a built-in tension between two worthy objectives. On one hand, every professor needs to exert enough control over class discussion to ensure that the students are exposed to the key points embedded in the lesson. On the other hand, we want to leave the discussion sufficiently free that our students can discover those points on their own. If we cut off the discussion too readily, jumping in to summarize all the key points before the students have had time to absorb them, they will gain only a superficial understanding and will feel no ownership in the lessons learned. But if we let the discussion run on and on, some students will be left confused and dismayed, unable to extract from the lesson what you wanted them to learn. As a new teacher, you will likely feel a strong impulse to be *overly* controlling of class discussion — using leading questions to prod the students toward your desired conclusion, abruptly correcting the slightest misstep, interrupting an observation because it does not seem to be headed in the "right" direction. Our advice is to let the discussion run a little. Don't be afraid to draw out, with more questions, a student whose initial answer is wrong. Don't hesitate to encourage a back-and-forth debate between students who disagree about a key point. Don't be shy about pressing a student to be more precise even though her initial answer is basically correct. If the discussion veers off on a tangent, carrying the students far afield of the central points in your lesson, you'll have to step in and gently guide them back from their detour. But don't pounce on every off-topic remark. Give the discussion some breathing room.* In the end, leave yourself time to clarify and summarize the key points that you want them to get from the lesson.[146]

D. HOW TO HANDLE CLASS QUESTIONS

Our earlier exhortation to "play the role"[147] of a law school professor is especially apt when it comes to handling classroom questions. You want the students to find you ready, willing, and able to answer their questions. Particularly at the semester's outset, you don't want to inspire doubt in their minds about whether you know the material. But given the nightly struggle to prepare for class amid all your many distractions, there will come a time when, standing in breathless silence before your students, you won't have an answer. What should you do? It is OK to say, "Let me think about it." This buys you time — so you can scurry to the hornbooks that night and put together an answer for the next class session. Some professors will try to answer the question by thinking out loud, working through the problem to produce an answer on the spot. You should resist such an impulse. While standing at the board, puzzling over an unforeseen question, it is amazing how easily you can overlook the obvious applicability of a well-established rule. One of the worst things you can do in handling any issue, whether a student question or not, is to make an erroneous statement — because you *must* clean it up: in an e-mail message, or a TWEN posting, or at the very start of your next class. It's not the end of the world if you make a mistake, and you should always correct and clarify as soon as you can when you've done so, but those instances can be dramatically reduced by giving yourself time to reflect and, if necessary, to research.

What should be your general approach to answering classroom questions? Be respectful and empathetic toward the student. Approach the question with the presumption that it was asked in good faith and was triggered by genuine confusion. Why do we offer this advice? Because some questions will seem so incongruous, or will evince such a poor understanding of the concept you thought you had clearly conveyed, that you'll be startled, frustrated, and maybe even angry. Don't let this show. If you are by nature an impatient person, you must play the role of a patient teacher in the classroom.

Sometimes a question will pertain not to the material you're currently covering but to something that you'll reach in the near future. If this is true, say so. Pinpoint the section of your course to which the question pertains, ask the student to hold the question, and promise that you'll address it at the appropriate time. You should then scribble a note to yourself to preserve your memory of the question. You should

---

* Intervening, in an effort to encourage and channel rigorous analysis, may in fact stifle animated debate.

also ask the student to remind you of the question if you fail to answer it at the appropriate time. That will demonstrate your concern for the student's understanding of the material — and it will improve the likelihood that you'll actually remember to answer the question.

Some questions will raise issues that tie the current material to a topic that is way off in the future. This can be difficult to recognize if you are teaching the course for the first time. But if you have followed our advice on how to prepare for the semester, reading an overview that charts the full doctrinal trajectory of your course,[148] there is a good chance you'll spot the connection. Once you've taught the course a few times, it will be easy to identify the distant topic that the student's question has evoked. At this point, you have to make an on-the-spot decision: Do you defer the question until later, merely specifying which section of your course will address it, or do you briefly explain that distant material and offer an answer now? It is usually better to wait — unless you're convinced that the students will benefit from your digression rather than being confused by it.

Finally, don't let obscure questions bog down your class sessions. Though they are sometimes posed by show-offs, these questions often come from your most gifted students, and you don't want to discourage their interest. At the same time, you can't allow their curiosity to monopolize valuable class time. Inevitably, these questions pertain to minutiae that you would never test your students on. If that's the case, then simply say, "That's a great question, but it raises a finer point that I would never test you on, so let's talk about it after class." With this reply, you are demonstrating your respect for the student's interest while simultaneously quelling the anxiety that obscure questions trigger in some students.[149] If the question *does* explore an issue that is testable on your exam, then it *is* something you'll need to address in front of the whole class — the only question is *when*. If it squarely pertains to the material that you are covering right then, you probably ought to deal with it straight away. But if it's linked more closely to material down the road, then (consistent with our advice above) you'll want to hold off until the appropriate time.

E. HOW TO USE HYPOTHETICALS AND PROBLEMS

In teaching legal analysis, we believe that it's not enough to discuss the cases in your casebook, that it's not enough to probe those cases for the rules they contain, that it's not enough to mix in the occasional hypothetical. We believe that case analysis must be regularly supplemented with hypotheticals *and* problems — which we regard as having different forms and serving different purposes. As used here, a hypothetical is purely oral. It is best offered as a series of slightly different factual variations, and it is best used to illustrate the limits of one particular element in a cause of action or defense (for example, the *promise* element that must be proved by the plaintiff in a promissory estoppel action). We also strongly advocate the use of problems. A problem, in contrast to a hypothetical, is best presented to students in writing, usually in advance of the class session in which it is employed. A problem is best offered not with built-in factual variations, but as one concrete fact pattern, and it is best used not to illustrate one particular element, but to give the students practice in applying *all* of the elements that make up a cause of action or defense (even if it focuses attention on the one or two elements most in dispute).

Just to be certain that these terms are clear, let's look at the elements that comprise a promissory estoppel claim:

1. The defendant made a *promise*
2. that *induced*
3. an act of *detrimental reliance* by the plaintiff/promisee;
4. the promisee's reliance was *reasonable and foreseeable*; and
5. injustice can be avoided only by *enforcing* the promise.[150]

A hypothetical could be effectively employed to test the limits of the *promise* element — especially if the assigned readings for the day feature two or three cases that construe, and hinge upon, the requirements of that element.[151] If the students can be prompted to probe those cases for a detailed picture of the *promise* element, they will see that it requires the expression of an affirmative and unqualified commitment by the promisor — a requirement that cannot be satisfied if the promissory language is in any way optional, discretionary, or conditional. Once those requirements have been extracted from the case law, the students are ready for a hypothetical that will test their grasp of the *promise* element. A well-constructed hypothetical would feature multiple variations on the same basic promise, with subtle changes in the promissory language that cover the spectrum from clearly optional to clearly unconditional.

By contrast, a well-constructed problem would feature a single fact pattern and would require the students to state and apply *all* the elements of promissory estoppel. It would be reduced to writing, distributed to the students in advance, and would not be employed until their study of promissory estoppel reached its culmination.[152] In the classroom, the professor will push the students to walk through every step of their analysis — in exactly the same sequence, and with exactly the same level of detail, as if they were writing it on a final exam.

Why do we believe that hypotheticals and problems are *both* necessary? Because they are equally valuable but serve different purposes. By isolating one particular element and compelling its application to a range of factual variations, a hypothetical gives students a nuanced understanding of the requirements and limits of that element. Problems, on the other hand, are valuable because they reinforce the step-by-step nature of legal analysis, training students to identify all the elements in a cause of action and giving them practice applying those elements as they would on an exam.

How do you provide an ample supply of problems? You can always create them yourself — that's the best way to ensure that they're smoothly integrated into your course. But writing your own problems can be very time-consuming.[153] One alternative is to select a casebook that consistently features its own problems.[154] Or you might turn to the *Examples and Explanations* series, published by Aspen.[155] Each volume in this series is a mini-treatise, punctuated with well-crafted problems (and corresponding answers) that focus on key doctrinal points. These problems are relatively easy to incorporate into your course because they target specific rules and they are set forth in chapters that will likely correspond to the chapters in your casebook. Finally, you can supplement your inside-the-classroom problems with periodic homework assignments that direct your students to take computer-based CALI[156] exercises.*

F. SPECIAL TECHNIQUES FOR FIRST-YEAR STUDENTS

In our experience, the following techniques are useful when introducing first-year students to the rudiments of legal analysis.

1. "Case Dissection" Exercises: Teaching Legal Analysis by Breaking an Opinion Down into Its Component Parts

Many first-year students will struggle when asked to locate a particular passage in a judicial opinion — whether it be the holding, the rationale, or the court's effort to distinguish an earlier precedent. Students have trouble with such questions because they don't yet recognize the component parts that make up a judicial opinion. If you ask them to pinpoint a key passage in the court's analysis — inquiring, for example, what test the judge employs — some students will respond with language that comes from a completely different part of the court's opinion. They will focus, for example, not upon the court's legal analysis but on a much earlier passage in which the judge recounts the procedural posture or the arguments advanced by the parties. How is it possible for a student to be so far off target? They simply haven't learned how to break a case down into its component parts. They don't yet see that almost every case contains the following segments (not always in this order):[157]

1. Facts
2. Procedural Posture
3. Framing the Issues
4. Arguments Advanced by the Parties
5. Analysis (often includes rationale/policy)
6. Holding
7. Disposition

Early in the first semester, when your students are still getting accustomed to reading cases, it is well worth your time to identify these component parts and to train your students to recognize them. You can accomplish this while covering one or more of the assigned cases in your syllabus. When conducting a "case dissection" exercise, you are literally asking your students to take a judicial opinion and divide it

---

* Even if you do not incorporate problems into your course, you can still recommend to students that they work through problems outside of class. And you'll be doing your students a further favor by strongly suggesting that they write out the answers to at least some of the problems.

up — page by page, paragraph by paragraph — into its component parts. By carving up an opinion in this way, the students become more keenly aware of how a decision is structured. With such awareness, they find it much easier to navigate an opinion, locating and extracting important details. They also find it much easier to discern each step in a court's analytical path — opening their eyes to the building blocks of legal analysis.

By way of example, let's use *Embry v. Hargadine, McKittrick Dry Goods Company*,[158] a contract formation case that deals with the so-called meeting of the minds. A dissection of *Embry* produces the following breakdown (page numbers from the Southwestern Reporter appear in brackets):

1. Facts [777 to 778]
2. Procedural Posture [first paragraph on 778]
3. Framing the Issues [second paragraph on 778]
4. Analysis [third paragraph on 778 through first paragraph on 780]
5. Disposition [second paragraph on 780]

After the students have identified the component parts of an opinion, you should push them to dissect the Analysis section, retracing and describing each step taken by the judge. In *Embry*, the court's analysis proceeds in five basic steps. First, the court addresses Issue No. 1 — whether contract formation is governed by an objective or subjective test — setting forth the governing law and its underlying policy [778-779]. Second, the court announces its holding as to Issue No. 1 — contract formation is governed by an *objective* test [779]. Third, the court turns to Issue No. 2 — whether plaintiff's version of events satisfies the test for contract formation [779]. Fourth, the court applies the objective test to plaintiff's factual allegations [779-780]. Fifth and finally, the court announces its holding on Issue No. 2 — if the facts took place as plaintiff alleges, then as a matter of law the parties *did* achieve contract formation [780].

This is very basic stuff. It may seem almost too fundamental to spend time on in class. But first-year students really benefit from it. By devoting some time to it early in the first semester, you will save yourself from having to offer remedial instruction down the road.

2. Legal Analysis from the Top Down and the Bottom Up

First-year students must be trained to formulate an analytical "game plan" for every issue on which they might be tested. Since different issues are governed by different rules and precedents, every analytical game plan will be unique in its particulars — but in formulating these game plans, students must be given a basic approach that they can follow time and time again. We offer such an approach. It comprises the first step in a two-step conception of legal analysis that proceeds, as we describe it, "from the top down and the bottom up." Here is how it works.

In our experience, first-year students find it helpful to think of legal analysis as proceeding in two fundamental steps. The first step — "top down" — is to spot a given issue (by looking at the facts closely enough to figure out what issues may be in play), and then to assemble the legal framework for analyzing it, starting from a big-picture perspective (the general subject area or doctrine that governs the issue) and then adding layers of detail (identifying the applicable rule, breaking it down into elements, and then using the case law to fill in the finer points of each element). Then the facts are examined to determine whether they satisfy each of those elements.[159] Only after this "top down" approach has been performed (applying facts to rules) should a student proceed to step two ("bottom up") — focusing at a micro level on the factual details to see if they suggest the applicability of any legal issues that might have been overlooked during the "top down" process. Essentially, "bottom up" means retracing your steps with a fine-tooth comb, sifting the factual details for any issue you might have missed.

Left unguided, many students will gravitate toward a haphazard variation of "bottom up," with no "top down" counterpart. They'll blow through the facts, hanging legal labels on some of them, but they'll miss entire sub-issues that would have been evident in a "top down," step-by-step analysis. And if a key fact implicates two different issues, they tend to spot only one of those issues because they normally assign only one label to any given fact.

The goal here is to guide students away from quick, conclusory characterizations of facts to an understanding that legal analysis is about recognizing the requirements of a particular rule and then, in step-by-step fashion, demonstrating that the rule is or is not met. We believe that students need lots of practice performing this two-step process in the classroom, particularly through the use of problems (as described above[160]) that focus on the legal doctrines they have just learned.

Let's take a closer look at step one — spotting the issue and erecting the legal framework (the "game plan") for analyzing it. We advise our students to start from the broadest big-picture perspective and to zero in, more and more specifically, on the applicable doctrine, the governing rule, the elements of that rule, and the finer points of each element. To illustrate, let's say that we've been given a fact pattern in which the plaintiff is seeking to enforce a promise made to him by the defendant. Since we're dealing with the enforceability of a promise, we are probably in the realm of contract law. The facts offer no indication of mutual assent or consideration, but it does appear that the plaintiff relied on the promise and suffered injury because of that reliance. Thus, within the realm of contract law, it appears that we're looking at a promissory estoppel issue. So what do we know about promissory estoppel? To begin with, we know how it's defined:

> A promise which the promisor should reasonably expect to induce action or forbearance on the part of the promisee or a third person and which does induce such action or forbearance is binding if injustice can be avoided only by enforcement of the promise.[161]

Rules like this are too dense, too unwieldy for precise application when sifting through the facts. Any rule that contains multiple requirements, clustered together in a single block of text, is all too susceptible to misapplication. If the individual requirements do not stand out separately and clearly, they are easily blurred or overlooked. Accordingly, we urge our students to break down every doctrine, rule, cause of action, or defense[162] into separate, specific requirements — *elements* — so that it's easier to single out the facts that pertain to each requirement. These elements essentially serve as *questions* to be asked of the fact pattern. (Did the defendant make a *promise* to the plaintiff? Did the plaintiff *rely* on that promise?) Promissory estoppel's dense definition can be reduced to five concise elements (as set forth in our earlier discussion of hypotheticals and problems[163]). Those elements will comprise the basic structure of our analytical game plan, but they do not suffice by themselves. Now we must push the students to dig deeper, to extract from the case law any lessons they learned about the finer points of each element. As an illustration, let's use (once again[164]) the *promise* element of promissory estoppel. Standing by itself, the word *promise* does not tell us how strictly or loosely we should interpret this requirement. But the case law does tell us. The modern cases make clear that *promise* requires the expression of an affirmative and unqualified commitment, in language offering no suggestion that the promisor's obligation is optional or discretionary.[165]

This interpretation of the *promise* element must be added to our analytical game plan.[166] Likewise, we must add to our game plan any comparable interpretations, glosses, or limitations that the case law has imposed on the other elements of promissory estoppel, as well as any "gray areas" (commonly disputed situations or borderline applications). By incorporating these finer points from the case law, we have given the elements a more accurate and sharply defined form. Policy arguments can also be added, those specific to a particular doctrine and those of more general applicability.[167] Ultimately, by going through this exercise, the student is prompted to recall, in an organized and useable manner, everything that she has learned about the given topic. In other words, she is prompted to identify everything the legal system considers relevant to the analysis of this problem, so that she can look at the facts and see more clearly whether they satisfy the governing elements. In effect, the "top down" approach tells students what questions they need to ask of the facts, just as it would tell an attorney what questions to ask of her client.

Thus, after working our way through step one, we have produced a detailed legal framework for analyzing the facts in our promissory estoppel problem. The "top down" approach can be used by students to create analytical game plans for any legal issue. They can use the approach whenever they're required to perform legal analysis on the spot; it helps them to stay organized and to proceed in an orderly fashion. The approach can also be used in advance of exams, enabling students to prepare analytical game plans for any of the issues on which they might be tested.

We recommend this approach not only because it's helpful to students, but because it's employed by the best trial lawyers, who always reduce their claims and defenses to elements.[168] This simply underscores the fact that legal analysis (as we observed earlier[169]) is always the same enterprise — in the classroom, the law office, and the courtroom. The facts will come to us in varying levels of detail and uncertainty, the rules in different degrees of clarity and "settledness," but in the end legal analysis always entails identifying the governing rule and sifting the facts to determine whether they satisfy that rule. Breaking the rule into elements simply makes it easier to achieve a complete and accurate meshing of law and facts.

G. RIGHT AFTER CLASS, MAKE NOTES OF WHAT DID AND DIDN'T WORK

The best way to improve as a teacher is to learn from your mistakes and your successes in the classroom — and the best time to record those lessons is right after you experience them, when the details are still fresh in your mind. These notes will be particularly valuable if you keep careful track of exactly what you were covering when the incident occurred. Be sure to consult them the next time you teach that course, reading all of them before the semester begins and then following their progression on a week-by-week basis.

VII. Using Technology to Support Your Teaching[170]

A. VISUAL AIDS IN THE CLASSROOM

The classroom experience in law school is a verbal ping-pong match, with words and ideas bouncing off the walls. In this environment, the lesson to be learned is all too elusive, and a student can quickly lose track of what's important. How can you alleviate this problem? By providing some *visual reinforcement* of the topic or theme or point you're covering. By *visual* we don't necessarily mean *pictorial*; the visual reinforcement we're talking about usually takes the form of a few *words*, written on the board or projected from a PowerPoint slide. Those words function like agenda items for a meeting, helping to anchor and clarify the content of the discussion. If students are momentarily distracted, those agenda items will help them to recapture the thread of your discussion. By communicating with the students not only through their ears but also through their eyes, you increase their ability to grasp and retain the content of your presentation.[171]

How much visual reinforcement should you provide? On this question there is abundant room for personal preference. A good rule of thumb is to update your message each time you progress to a new topic, theme, or point. The difficulty is deciding how much *detail* to provide — in other words, how densely phrased should your message be? If your aim is to insert very specific language right into your students' notes, then presenting that language verbatim is probably the way to go.

But remember what you're creating here — it's the *visual* reinforcement of aurally conveyed details, so you should err on the side of *compact* expression. Your message will better serve its visual purpose, and your students will find it easier to digest, if you express it as a phrase or clause or topic heading.

The oldest "visual aid," writing in chalk on a blackboard, has advantages and disadvantages. Its greatest virtues are spontaneity and flexibility — giving you the readiness to pounce immediately on any idea at any time in any sequence. But most teachers have terrible handwriting that is made even worse by their hurry in throwing it onto the board. Even when the handwriting is excellent, a chalky script is difficult to see from any distance. Viewed from the back row of a large classroom, the blackboard itself can look like a postage stamp. Thus, in some law school classrooms, the blackboard's utility is negated from the outset. (This underscores the importance of visiting your assigned classroom well before the semester begins; you may find that the room itself is hostile to your plans for visual aids.) Another problem with the blackboard is that many items well worth sharing with your students — a chart, a quotation, a statute — will be too time-consuming to write out during class. You can show up twenty-five minutes before class and write out every word of a detailed chart or a lengthy text, but it will never be as visible or legible as a PowerPoint slide.

With PowerPoint, you lose the spontaneity and sequential freedom of the blackboard,[172] but you gain a sharp, clear image that can be magnified to suit the largest classrooms. You also gain the ability to create charts and diagrams; to display photographs (which can be useful, *inter alia*, in humanizing long-dead Supreme Court justices or illustrating the real-world background of a case); and to highlight key clauses in a statute, a judicial decision, a contract, or a will. Another advantage is that you can insert a hyperlink on a PowerPoint slide that will transport you and your students to a specific website. So, for example, if you are teaching Civil Procedure students about jury trials, you can jump from a PowerPoint slide directly to the website of a federal district court, where you can show your students the standing jury trial orders that govern civil cases in that district.[173] Or, just as easily, you could jump to the website of a company that manufactures cross-examination software, which can be used to store and display video clips from the deposition of an opposing witness if he deviates from that testimony at trial.[174]

PowerPoint can help to alleviate a problem that law students have always faced: the impossible challenge of producing class notes that are accurate and complete. How can they distill the verbal ping-pong match that reverberates in every classroom? Even a seasoned court reporter would be strained by the effort. Inevitably, many students produce class notes in which key concepts are distorted or garbled — a problem that stems from their harried efforts to transcribe the flurry of utterances blowing past them. If all they are doing in class is scrambling to write down what's being said, they are learning next to nothing. They are simply recording sentence fragments, not processing ideas. The mere use of PowerPoint does not necessarily ease this problem; students will find it just as difficult to copy a detailed slide as a long-winded utterance. But the problem is greatly reduced if, shortly after class, the professor *gives* the PowerPoint slides to her students. (This can be done by posting the slides on a password-protected Web page.) By giving them the slides, we are giving them a skeleton, an outline of what we covered in class that day. If the students know that they'll receive the outline right after class, they are released from the burden of being court reporters and they are freed to listen and absorb what's important. Now, guided by the slides in class, they can focus their note-taking on the finer points. They will take fewer but better notes — and those notes will serve as interstices to the basic outline furnished by the slides.

We come, finally, to videos and DVDs. These have special value in the Evidence and Civil Procedure courses, where courtroom dramas can serve as vivid illustrations of jury selection, opening statements, direct and cross-examination, hearsay exceptions, impeachment techniques, and closing arguments. A number of casebook authors, including Mueller and Kirkpatrick,[175] provide DVDs containing film clips for which they have secured copyright permission.[176] In the First Amendment and Constitutional Law courses, excerpts from historical dramas and documentaries can help students better appreciate the context in which key cases were decided. When using any of these materials, of course, special care must be taken to comply with the copyright laws.

Much has been written on the use of visual aids in legal education, but the articles by Paul Wangerin[177] and Robert E. Oliphant[178] are especially worth reading.

B. CREATING A WEB PAGE FOR YOUR CLASS

When students arrive at law school, they are already well accustomed to obtaining information from the Internet. In their own educational experience, they have probably been using websites since their high school days to get reading assignments and course information from their teachers. So they will likely expect a Web page to exist for each of their law school courses. You're free to disappoint them, of course, but don't reject the use of a Web page until you've considered its advantages.

The primary advantage of a course Web page is that it gives you an efficient means of conveying to your students detailed information about your course. A skeptical reply might be: "I already have a well-established means of conveying course information to my students — it's called a *syllabus*." True enough, but in an age of electronic information, today's student does not cling to paper like those of earlier generations. Four weeks after you've given each student a hard copy of your syllabus, half of them will have lost it. A skeptical response might be: "Too bad for them. That's not *my* problem." But it *will* be your problem when you have to field a multitude of e-mails and phone calls inquiring about the current reading assignment, or whether your exam is open-book or closed-book, or any other information that you carefully included in your now-vanished syllabus. Ultimately, the advantage of a course Web page is that it's convenient for your students *and for you* if all of the important information about your course is available at one specific location on the Internet. Once your students know that a Web page exists for your course, they will rarely bother you with administrative questions. Instead, they will fall into the comfortable habit, inculcated since high school, of getting their course information from the Internet.

A course Web page usually consists of menu items — e.g., "Syllabus," "Problems for In-Class Analysis," etc. — that function as hyperlinks. So, for example, if the student clicks on "Syllabus," she'll be transported immediately to the posted copy of your syllabus. Any electronic file can be posted. Web page postings routinely include WordPerfect and Microsoft Word documents, PDF files, and PowerPoint presentations. Your menu items can also function as hyperlinks to other *websites*. Thus, a Civil Procedure Web page might include a menu item linked to the U.S. Courts website, transporting students to a map of the federal circuit and district court boundaries.[179]

A Web page need not be a complex, labor-intensive albatross for the professor. Even if you merely posted your syllabus there, and did nothing more, your Web page would afford you all of the administrative advantages discussed above. Moreover, it isn't necessary that *you* post anything; at any law school, someone on staff will be able to do that for you. If you want to post a new item, all you have to do is e-mail it to the person who is helping you. Likewise, if you want to create a hyperlink to a website, simply give your assistant the relevant Web address. Your only remaining task would be to specify the wording of the new menu item. Given the simplicity of these steps, you could painlessly inaugurate a course Web page by posting a single document — your syllabus. Eventually, you might make a practice of posting anything that you pass out in the classroom (problems, charts, etc.). These modest measures will be greatly appreciated by your students. Thus, a Web page can be a simple, no-frills affair, with no duty falling upon the professor to edit or maintain it.

At the other end of the spectrum, a professor can easily expand the range of offerings on her Web page, using software that facilitates direct, hands-on control. Using TWEN,[180] Blackboard,[181] or Contribute,[182] you will find it easy to edit or update your Web page, giving you the freedom to post or delete items whenever you wish — without having to ask for technical assistance. With this new-found independence, you can turn your Web page into a conduit of information and resources related to your course.[183] So, for example, one of us expanded his Civil Procedure Web page to include an entire library of real-world pleadings and motions — complaints, answers with counterclaims, motions to dismiss, motions to transfer venue, discovery requests, deposition notices, motions for summary judgment, proposed jury instructions — more than thirty in all, taken from his own past cases and those of distinguished contributors. Why do this? Because first-year students have no idea what a complaint or a summary judgment motion looks like. By giving them some concrete examples, he hopes to demystify the litigation process and to paint a clearer picture of a lawsuit's many stages. To share these materials with your students, it isn't *essential* to have a Web page — it would be easy enough to place hard copies on reserve in the law library — but the convenience for students is infinitely greater if you post them on the Web. Now students can browse them at any time of the day or night, whether they're at home or at a coffee house or in an airport terminal. And this reinforces the whole reason for making the materials available in the first place: When a student sits down to read her first summary judgment assignment — when she reads Rule 56 for the first time and says to herself (like so many students before her), "What in the world does *that* mean?" — she should be able to go *immediately* to your sample summary judgment motions to get a sense of the Rule's operation. In other words, you want her to have access to those samples at the very moment when her curiosity is piqued, no matter where she is, no matter when it happens. She shouldn't have to make a special trip downtown to visit the law library. This is the beauty of the course Web page — it encourages you to assemble resources for your students because it makes those resources so readily accessible.

Just as a course Web page promotes the delivery of course-related resources, so it facilitates the distribution of an expanded package of teaching materials. Your Web page can serve as a repository of problems and exercises that you've created for the course; it can house each PowerPoint presentation you've given, arrayed sequentially using the date of the class session in which it appeared; and you can post judicial decisions there that do not appear in your casebook but that you want to assign as supplemental reading. Here is an example of how posting certain teaching materials on a Web page can make them easier for the professor to implement and easier for the students to use. The materials were created for a mock deposition in the Civil Procedure course that one of us teaches. That deposition is the culminating step in covering the discovery process, and it serves as a bridge to covering summary judgment. The deposition takes place in the context of a hypothetical lawsuit that stems from a failed business venture involving two corporations. One of those companies is now suing the other for fraud, breach of contract, and promissory estoppel. In the deposition, the professor plays the role of the plaintiff's star witness, its CEO. Students assigned to the defense team ask questions of the witness. Their questioning is not random; each student is given a particular objective, and the team's overarching goal is to elicit testimony that will set up a defense motion for summary judgment. Another group of students is assigned to the plaintiff. They take turns sitting next to the witness and objecting, where appropriate, to the questions posed by the defense lawyers. To make the experience richer and more realistic, the professor fabricated a dozen exhibits — a signed contract, an earlier draft of the disputed contractual clause, interoffice memoranda that circulated among key players inside the plaintiff corporation, and letters sent to and from the parties. At the deposition, the defense lawyers are permitted, but not required, to introduce any of those exhibits while questioning the witness. The professor also created three other documents to be used by the students as background information for this exercise: a memorandum setting forth the basic, undisputed facts; a timeline specifying the exact dates of certain events in the case; and a chart listing the elements of plaintiff's claims. Distributing those fifteen documents in hard copy to more than sixty students would have been burdensome, chaotic, and wasteful. But it was a simple matter to post them on the course Web page, listing each document as a separate menu item and thereby making it separately viewable and downloadable. Here a course Web page facilitated the distribution of ambitious teaching materials, paving the way for a learning experience that students found valuable. Absent a Web page, the logistical burden of delivering those materials might have compromised or thwarted the experience.

Finally, a course Web page is the perfect place to post audio files of your classroom lectures for purposes of *podcasting*.[184] Podcasting is still relatively novel, and many law schools are still weighing its pros and cons,[185] but CALI is working to make it inexpensive and widely available through its Classcaster[186] project. If you do decide to employ podcasting, your course Web page is the logical place to post your audio files.

VIII. Conducting the Course Review Session

Try to reserve the semester's final class period for a course review session. There are three basic ways to conduct a course review: (1) confining it to a question-and-answer session; (2) delivering a lecture that sums up everything you covered, but leaving some time at the end to take questions; or (3) working through one of your old exams. Let's briefly examine each of these alternatives.

The Question-and-Answer Session: Of the three formats, this is the easiest for the professor, but there is little else to recommend it. The only real virtue of a strict questions-only format is that it directly targets those areas that the students are concerned about, since it only covers those topics that the students specifically raise. It doesn't waste fifteen minutes covering topics that the students find easy (which can happen with a summarizing lecture). But there are serious drawbacks here. By putting the onus on the students, this format produces lots of awkward silences. Students (particularly first-year students) tend to be shy about asking questions because they don't want to appear "stupid." If they do summon the courage to ask one question, they are loath to ask another, even though they might be genuinely confused about more than one topic. These sessions never fill an entire class period, and when they conclude (or, more precisely, when they peter out), the room feels heavy with bottled-up questions. One partial solution is to solicit questions in advance (submitted by e-mail). This may elicit a longer list, but if you ever poll your students, asking them which of the three formats they want for their review session, the question-and-answer session never wins.

The Summarizing Lecture: This is a far more labor-intensive format for the professor, but students tend to find it much more satisfying — especially if the lecture is accompanied by PowerPoint slides. If you began the semester with a Goodyear Blimp Overview,[187] you can follow the same flight path here, but now you'll be reviewing the rules at a greater level of detail. Professors sometimes underestimate the helpfulness of these lectures, probably because they are so familiar with the subject and so conscious of how they have structured the course. But for many students, this lecture is not merely a useful recapitulation of the rules; it marks the first time that they really *see* how all the pieces fit together. By performing a combination of the first and second formats, you can ameliorate some of the limitations of each. But one drawback of either format is that it leaves the students with only a passive role to play. It does not give them any practice analyzing a fact pattern with the rules they've learned. In short, it does not get them doing what they'll have to do on your exam. That defect is remedied by the next format.

Working Through One of Your Old Exams: This is the format that students like best *after* they've gone through it; they usually pick the summarizing lecture if asked to state their preference in advance. Why do they like this format? Because it gives them a sense of what it will be like to take your exam — and it deepens their understanding of the rules by offering guidance on how to apply them. This method of review is helpful to students in preparing for either essay-style or short-answer exams. The key is to make sure that your old exam is set up in the same style as the new exam you're planning to give. For best results, give your students a copy of the old exam at least one week before your review session. Then, as you work your way through the exam, be sure to call on students constantly to keep their level of involvement high. Your goal here should always be the same — prompting your students to identify and explain, step by step, how they would analyze the questions presented by the exam. If you spent class time during the semester working through practice exams or problems, there is arguably less need for this type of final review. Still, active review is always more effective than passive review, and the students are always grateful to conclude the semester with an experience that acquaints them with the format and requirements of your exam.

IX. The Sensitive Interval Between the Final Class and the Day of the Exam

When the semester comes to a close and your final class session is over, you will feel a great sense of relief. If you're a new teacher, you'll probably imagine that your students are sealing themselves off in air-tight seclusion where they'll remain, incommunicado, until the day of the exam. "Fine," you'll think, "now I can have some peace and quiet while I write my exam." Nothing could be further from the truth. You will suddenly find yourself as popular and pursued as a Hollywood starlet. If, all semester long, nobody bothered to visit during your office hours, you'll be appalled by your new-found celebrity. Year after year, the end of the final class session triggers a burst of passionate interest in your course — especially among your least mature students. Brace yourself for their questions, which often display a staggering unfamiliarity with your course. Such questions, coming at the end of a semester in which you pushed yourself to be helpful and accessible, can be dispiriting, annoying, infuriating. Thus, the interval between the final class session and the day of the exam is a period that is fraught with danger for any professor. This is when you can really lose your temper. And this is when, while making an effort to be generous with your time, you can inadvertently bestow an advantage upon the students who may be least deserving of your aid. What about the students who quietly retire to the library and prepare for the exam without ever asking you a single question? They don't receive any of the extra counseling that you lavish on the less industrious students who flock to your door. Is that fair?

We are troubled by the possibility that any student might gain an edge on the exam by extracting from the professor, after the final class session, an explication or clarification that is never communicated to the rest of the students. One of us, regretting it all the while, has continued to make himself fully available to students throughout the reading period. But the other has experimented with a policy that scrupulously avoids these "*ex parte*" communications with students. He would make a series of announcements — in the first week of class and then several more times as the semester's end approaches — telling the students that after the final class session he will not discuss the exam with any of them. This policy (which he calls "the gag rule") strikes some of his colleagues as overly severe. But we'd like you to know his reasons for adopting it.

There are two basic advantages to the gag rule. It forces students to engage in ongoing review, so that they don't wait until the eve of the exam to assess their understanding of the material. And it protects the professor from any accusation that he gave favored treatment to a particular student in the final days leading up to the exam. Let's take a closer look at each of these advantages.

Many students arrive in law school without any appreciation of the need to perform an ongoing review, throughout the semester, of the material they are learning — and to seek immediate help from their professor as soon as they realize that they lack an adequate grasp of any given topic or doctrine. This is probably because, as undergraduates, they were always able to get away with last-minute cramming. So they fail to realize that such an approach can lead to disaster in law school. Accordingly, students should be cautioned that they must not wait until after the final class session to figure out whether they understand a semester's worth of material. And a mere exhortation is not enough; some type of *disincentive* must be added to the mix. This is the reason for the gag rule. It encourages ongoing review by penalizing the student who fails to review until after classes have ended. By announcing the rule several times during the semester, you put the students on notice that the last-minute question will not be answered — at least not by you. Though admittedly harsh, such a rule may be necessary to break some students of the cramming habit that took hold of them in their undergraduate days.

The gag rule's other advantage is that it places the professor beyond suspicion that she may have given someone a last-minute edge on her exam. Long before he adopted the gag rule, one of us noticed a colleague who spoke to many students during the reading period but failed to employ a consistent approach in answering their questions. This professor got the same question from multiple students — and gave different answers depending on how much he liked the student who asked it. You don't have to be a malevolent person to fall into this trap. It is human nature to be willing to spend more time answering the student who seems genuinely lost, especially if that student apparently spent a long time searching for the answer before approaching you, rather than the student who is clearly trying to cut corners. Your natural inclination will be to lavish more attention and assistance upon the diligent student — perhaps furnishing a more detailed or nuanced reply — while giving a perfunctory answer to the lazy student. You must always strive to avoid this disparity of treatment. If it happens early in the semester, you have time to rectify it — but if it happens on the eve of the exam, there is a much greater risk that it will give the favored student an unfair advantage. The risk of harm is especially pronounced if a student comes to you during the reading period and asks you a question that is actually on your exam. Now it's within your power to give that student a complete, detailed answer — an answer that, if repeated in full on your exam, could easily improve the student's grade. It must be admitted that this scenario does not always lead to a higher grade for the student.[188] But sometimes it does — the student will see you the day after the exam and mention how odd it was that the topic you two had been talking about was right there in the test. Either way, you will always feel a queasy sensation when a student asks you a question that you know will be on the exam. (Needless to say, the key is not to let on.) But why allow yourself to be placed in that situation? Why put yourself at risk of bestowing an unfair advantage upon any student? This is the principal benefit of the gag rule. It lifts you out of that compromising situation in which a few stray words of advice can tarnish the impartiality that you worked all semester to establish. And it means that you won't have to spend the entire reading period carefully rationing the guidance you give to every student who approaches you, taking care never to bestow too much help or too many insights upon any individual.

The gag rule's primary concern — making sure that you don't give some students an unfair advantage on the exam by favoring them during the reading period with explications or clarifications that are never communicated to the rest of the class — can be satisfied without imposing an absolute blackout on student questions. This can be done by requiring that all student questions during the reading period be communicated to you via e-mail, and by using a listserv to send both the question and your answer to the entire class, taking care not to reveal the identities of the students who sent in questions.

X. Creating the Exam[189]

One of the first questions you'll face when creating an exam is what *format* to use. Will it be essay, short answer, multiple choice, or some combination thereof? Essay is the traditional and presumptive format, at least for substantive courses, because it is best at testing the analytical skills that are the centerpiece of any law school education.[190] The short answer format may be better suited to rules courses like Evidence[191] and Civil Procedure.[192] This is because the application of a procedural rule (like the restriction on leading questions during the direct examination of a witness[193]) does not normally require the same extended analysis that would be necessary in applying a substantive doctrine (like deciding whether a state statute offends the Equal Protection Clause[194]). The multiple choice format has become more popular in recent years,[195] prompting a scholarly debate on its pros and cons.[196] Critics bemoan its growing acceptance,[197] arguing that essay exams are necessary for training students how to perform legal analysis[198] and surmising that the real attraction of multiple choice exams is that they are quick and easy to grade.[199] An eloquent proponent of the multiple choice format acknowledges that "I am not comfortable assigning grades based solely on performance on multiple choice [questions]," in part because an exclusive reliance on multiple choice "would not test certain of the skills I try to teach (for example, coming up with each party's arguments about how tort doctrines apply to a complex fact pattern)."[200] Thus, multiple choice is best employed as one component of an exam that also features a substantial reliance on the essay format.[201] If you decide to rely primarily on multiple choice or short answer questions, you may have to alter the way that you *cover* the material in the classroom. This is because multiple choice and short answer questions tend to be more sharply focused, more finely tuned, than a typical essay question — so if you're planning to *test* your students at a heightened level of precision, you'll need to *teach* them at a heightened level of precision.[202]

When selecting the issues to be tested on your exam, strive to identify a faithful sampling of the topics that comprised your course, and resist the impulse to cover everything. In short, try to be representative, not comprehensive. This is particularly advisable if you will be using an essay format. An essay exam designed to test every doctrine featured in the course could never be fair to the students — it would take them ten hours to complete. With a short answer or multiple choice format, you can cover more topics — but what you gain in coverage, you lose in your ability to see your students' analysis. The short answer format requires only a truncated analysis by the student; the multiple choice format gives you the student's conclusion and nothing more. There is one way to get a bit more coverage while still requiring a significant analytical performance from your students. This can be done by creating "directed" essay questions, which focus narrowly on a specific issue (e.g., "Is there an *offer* here?"). This is a far cry from the typical essay question, which is embedded with multiple issues and asks the student to analyze all the rights and duties of the parties. One drawback of the directed essay question is that the professor is essentially spotting the issue for the students,[203] but the format enables the professor to cover a broader range of topics while still affording a detailed picture of the student's analytical skills.[204] Ultimately, no matter what format you adopt, your goal in creating an exam should not be to achieve comprehensive coverage of every topic embraced by your course. Instead, your goal should be to incorporate a representative sampling of topics, and to devise a format that gives your students a fair opportunity to demonstrate their substantive mastery and analytical skill.[205]

When striving to be "representative, not comprehensive," there are several points to bear in mind. First, in selecting the issues to be tested, be sure to draw them from widely scattered sections of the course. Avoid a concentration of related topics. Second, be careful not to accord disproportionate scoring weight to a topic on which you spent comparatively little time during the semester. Thus, if you spent one class session covering UCC § 2-207 (the "battle of the forms"), that topic should not comprise half the total points on your exam. Third, you should strongly resist putting anything on the exam to which you devoted only a few fleeting minutes of classroom time. Fourth, be sure to design the exam in a manner strictly consistent with any statements or promises that you made to the students. Thus, if you told the students that your exam would focus solely upon the application of doctrinal rules, with no points to be awarded for discussions of policy, then you must be true to your word.[206]

If you choose to give an essay exam, you should strongly consider creating a detailed grading key to help you maintain consistency in scoring. We believe that consistency is impossible to achieve if the professor's discretion is not restricted by a self-imposed rubric[207] or grading key that identifies a specific range of points to be awarded for specific observations (in issue-spotting and analysis) by the student. (Though we offer a separate section, immediately below, on grading the exam,[208] we believe that creating the grading key is an integral part of creating the exam, so we address the subject here.) We just don't believe that it's possible for a professor, while reading an essay exam, to hold in her head all of the accumulating strengths and weaknesses of the student's performance, and to reduce those myriad impressions to a single summarizing score that will prove consistent when compared to the performances and scores of the other students. This "gut-reaction" approach overestimates the professor's ability to hold a multitude of variables in her head, to give each particular variable the same weight on every exam, and to maintain consistency and proportionality in awarding grades from the first exam to the last. To be frank, this is not humanly possible. The only way to approach these ideals is to create a scoring system in which each student is awarded a specific number of points for spotting a particular issue, recognizing the applicability of a particular line of precedent, or performing a particular analysis.[209]

New teachers tend to make their essay exams far too complicated, loading them with more issues than the students can handle or filling them with a bewildering factual complexity. The result is that the students are not given a fair chance to show what they've learned, and the teacher winds up having to spend an inordinate amount of time grading the exam. With your first few exams, you'll be surprised to find that many students won't even see the issues that you thought were obvious, and they'll be completely overmatched by the more challenging aspects of the test. Thus, when constructing an exam it is best to include a majority of items that were expressly covered in class, mixing in some new applications and a few doctrinal gray areas to give the better students some opportunities to distinguish themselves. After creating your exam, you should immediately construct a grading key or model answer — because doing so will make you more keenly aware of the exam's level of difficulty, at a point in time when you can still make some adjustments. If you put this task off until after your students have taken the exam, it will be too late to fix any flaws you discover. So get your grading key on paper and look at it critically. Are there too many issues? Too few? Any glaring omissions? Will any significant issue-spotting or analysis turn on a factual distinction too obscure for many students to discern? Will a large number of points be unavailable to a student who reasonably elects not to go down a particular path (and thus fails to discuss the sub-issues to which that path led)? If so, then adjust the exam accordingly, adding or subtracting issues or facts as needed. After teaching for a number of years, you'll get a feeling for these judgments. A good rule of thumb — for all teachers, but especially for new ones — is that it's always best to err on the side of fewer issues and less complexity.

Just as you'll likely underestimate how *difficult* your exam will be for students, so you will likely underestimate how much *time* they'll need to complete it. They don't have your command of the subject, so they can't be expected to devour the issues as readily as you could.[210] Over the years, we have grown increasingly generous in the time we allow for our exams. Imposing a hurried, harried pace is hardly the best way to measure a student's substantive grasp and analytical prowess.[211] Of course, the more time you give them, the more they'll write — leaving you with a taller stack of exams to grade.[212] But grading exams is part of your job, and you can't allow your distaste for it to distort the testing process. We worry that page limits and word limits likewise stem more from an aversion to grading than from any sound pedagogical purpose.[213] Taking your exam should not be like writing a haiku — the students should be focused on crafting the best analysis they can muster, not on reducing it to seventeen syllables or any other arbitrary limit.

Will your exam be open book or closed book? Each format has advantages and disadvantages. The closed book format is probably better at forcing students to learn the material. It requires them to "pull the course together" — mastering the key doctrines, forming a clear picture of how they interrelate, and memorizing the black-letter rules. The open book, open notes format often gives students a false sense of security, prompting them to prepare for the test less thoroughly. Many students fail to realize that they won't have *time* during the exam for much more than a fleeting glance at their books and notes. Thus, one of the key advantages of the open book format — that it causes students to approach the exam with less anxiety — turns out to be illusory once the exam gets underway. The main argument in favor of open book exams is that books and notes are *available* to lawyers in the real world so it's unfair to withhold them during the testing process. There are two answers to this argument. First, the *bar* exam is a closed book exam, so the closed book format better prepares students for the real-world trauma of the licensing process. Second, a real-world lawyer must be able to spot issues *without* looking at books or notes. If a client asks you to enforce a contract to purchase land, and then she acknowledges that the contract was never reduced to writing, you shouldn't have to consult a book to see that you've got a Statute of Frauds issue. At some point you'll have to research the case law in your jurisdiction, and *then*, of course, you'll need to open some books. But a good lawyer, like a good student, should have a mental storehouse of basic black-letter rules. This brings us to the main disadvantage of the closed book format: it precludes you from testing at a very specific, finely tuned level. You can expect your students to memorize the rules, but you can't expect them to memorize all the cases in your casebook. Thus, if you want their analysis to include a nuanced comparison of the exam facts with the factual details in the cases, you should adopt an open book format. Likewise, an open book format is probably appropriate for any course that centers upon a thick statutory code (e.g., Tax, UCC) or a dense compendium of rules (e.g., Evidence, Civil Procedure).[214]

When the time comes to create your exam, where can you turn for ideas? Helpful sources include recent cases, past bar exam questions, and ideas that occur to you during the semester. Let's say that you're teaching Contracts and you want to include a promissory estoppel issue on your exam. You might conduct a Lexis or Westlaw search for recent promissory estoppel cases. If you find one with good facts, you've got the raw material for an exam question. But don't just copy it exactly. You will probably have to simplify the facts and focus the issues, tailoring them to fit how *you* covered the subject. Bar examiners periodically publish their past exam questions, and these can serve as a fruitful source of ideas. Even a multiple choice question from the Multistate Exam can spark an idea for an essay question. But *never* duplicate anything taken from a published source, because some students may have encountered the question and will gain an unfair advantage. Another way to create a question is to begin with the *answer* already in mind and then, working backward, develop a set of facts which would yield that answer. Finally, the best exam ideas often come from notes that the professor jots down during the semester. The golden time for these notes is immediately after class, in reaction to something that happened during the discussion of a particular doctrine. The exam ideas that are generated inside the classroom are the best source of raw material for testing because they flow directly from the way that you taught the course.

XI. Grading the Exam

Young professors tend to obsess over grading, knowing that they have the fate of the students in their hands. They grade and re-grade. Recognize that if you have constructed a good grading key, you will arrive at the same or a very similar score every time you grade the same exam. As quality control, you can randomly select a few exams and grade them twice to see if this is true. Even if there is some variation in how you grade an exam the second time, a well-constructed grading key will prevent you from veering off in a markedly different direction. You might arrive at a different point total, but normally this won't produce more than a half-grade step in either direction. Such variations are inevitable and tend to even out over time.

If your exam is broken up into two or three different sections, each with its own fact pattern, the best approach is to grade one section at a time. There are two benefits to this approach. First, since your focus won't be interrupted by the fact patterns in the other sections, you'll find it easier to gauge the relative quality of each student's performance. Second, you'll be prevented from letting good or bad performance on one section influence your scoring of another, which is all too possible when you grade each student's exam all the way through.

If you follow the foregoing advice about multiple-section exams, you'll be taking multiple trips through your stack of bluebooks (a separate trip for each section of the exam), and this leads to another piece of advice. After your first trip through the stack, shuffle the exams into a new order, and do this before every subsequent trip through the stack. Why? Because exams that sit at the bottom of the stack are prone to suffer various forms of grading distortion. As a professor works through a stack of exams, the grades toward the bottom may trend up or down — down as the professor grows disappointed and therefore tougher; up if the professor starts to believe that nobody will hit the bull's eye and therefore becomes more generous.

It is also useful to grade at least several exams at each sitting to get rhythm and consistency — but this is less important if you have created a sufficiently precise scoring system. If, however, you employ the gut-reaction approach, it is really essential to grade a good number of exams at each sitting, because that approach can only hope to achieve consistency in scoring by juxtaposing one student's performance with another.[215]

Should the professor write comments and point scores directly on the student's exam or, instead, should the professor write them solely upon a separate score sheet (i.e., your grading key)? We recommend the latter. If you have created a good grading key, it will reveal very clearly how the student performed on the exam, so much so that you may find it unnecessary to add written comments. Adding written comments may be helpful to the professor in organizing her thoughts, and they will certainly be useful down the road if the student wants to talk about how she did, but the grading key will tell the tale quite clearly if you've done a good job creating it. Writing comments on every single exam can slow you down, and most students won't even bother looking at their exam, unless it's a mid-term or the midway point in a two-semester course. If you confine yourself to filling in points on a score sheet, you can move along expeditiously — yet at the same time you're creating a precise record of how the student performed.[216] This is why we suggest the so-called quick review session (described below[217]), to accommodate those students who want feedback without having to write comments on every single exam.

Let's turn to another advantage of using a separate score sheet. By recording the point scores only on your score sheet and not on the exam itself, you make it easier to change the points awarded if the topic turns out to be harder than you realized, warranting a readjustment of the allocated points. Now you won't have to scratch out the points you originally awarded, leaving alarming blots all over the student's exam. Students get anxious when they see this, wondering why the awarded points were changed. If you're only writing on a score sheet and not directly upon the student's exam, it's a simple matter to take out a clean copy of the revised score sheet and fill in the awarded points. During the review session, the professor can simply look at the score sheet to provide an overview of what the student did well and what could use some improvement.

XII. Reviewing the Exam

One way to review an exam is to schedule thirty-minute, one-on-one meetings with every student who wants to talk to you. If you do this, you'll find yourself repeating — again and again and *again* — the same basic information and advice. This is certainly a generous sacrifice of your time, but it's not necessarily the best format for every student. Many students want post-exam feedback, but most of them only have one or two questions. They neither want nor need a private, thirty-minute session — but they'll sign up for it if you don't offer any other opportunity for feedback. If exam review is to be helpful, it must be tailored to the actual needs and wishes of your students, affording a format for quick questions and a format for substantive feedback, while reserving the thirty-minute one-on-one session for the small remainder of students who really want it. Accordingly, we recommend a three-step approach to exam review, which proceeds as follows.

Step One is the "full" or "mandatory" review session ("mandatory" because we will not consent to a one-on-one office meeting with any student who fails to attend the full review). In this full review, the professor goes over the model answer or grading key, covering the main substance of the exam and answering any questions. This session could be replaced by simply posting the model answer or the grading key or the high A on your Web page — but we believe that this review is best performed in person, in order to encourage follow-up questions and to permit the back-and-forth exchanges that clarification often requires.

Step Two is the "quick review" session. The professor brings all of the exams into a classroom, lays them out on a long table, and allows the students to retrieve and examine their bluebooks. (One of us used to call this "the viewing," but the connotations of death associated with that term forced him to drop it.) The professor stays in the room to answer questions but does not give a lecture. There are several advantages to the quick review. First, some students are too intimidated to take the initiative to schedule a one-on-one office meeting with their professor, no matter how welcoming or approachable the professor may be. Here the invitation is conveyed by the professor, taking the onus off the student. A second advantage of the quick review is that it satisfies the needs of the vast majority of students, who merely want to flip through their bluebooks — reminding themselves of what they wrote, in light of the model answer — and perhaps ask one or two questions. Thus, when the quick review is over, most of your students will have no further questions and no further desire for feedback. But some students will want a deeper level of substantive explication — so for them we offer Step Three.

Step Three is the one-on-one office meeting, reserved for the few remaining students who were not satisfied by the "full" and "quick" reviews. It's here that you can pull out the student's exam and really focus on the virtues and flaws in her performance, offering detailed guidance on how to achieve a higher score. And it's here that you can provide remedial instruction to the student who missed the boat on one or more issues, who manifested a very poor grasp of a doctrine or concept, or who needs general advice on how to improve her analytical approach. These meetings are particularly appropriate for those students who finish at the very bottom of the class, but they are shyest of all when it comes to scheduling such a meeting. We often take the initiative to invite them, gently and unobtrusively, to come and see us, with a view toward bolstering their understanding and restoring their confidence.

XIII. Conclusion

We hope that the ideas contained in this book will prove helpful to new teachers entering the profession. We wrote this book primarily for them, though we hope that experienced teachers will find something useful in it. Over the course of our legal careers we have both played many roles — one of us in the legislative and executive branches, the other primarily in the courts — and in performing those labors we have found many satisfactions. But there is something special about teaching. After many years in the classroom, we still find it especially gratifying to help young people learn the law. It is our fondest hope that this book will be a resource for teachers who go on to experience, in their own careers, the inspiration and satisfaction that we have enjoyed.

Endnotes

1   The following bibliographies are excellent: Arturo L. Torres & Karen Harwood, *Moving Beyond Langdell: An Annotated Bibliography of Current Methods for Law Teaching*, 1994 GONZ. L. REV. 1 (spec. ed.); Arturo L. Torres & Mary Kay Lundwall, *Moving Beyond Langdell II: An Annotated Bibliography of Current Methods for Law Teaching*, 2000 GONZ. L. REV. 1 (spec. ed.); Arturo L. Torres, *McCrate Goes to Law School: An Annotated Bibliography for Teaching Lawyering Skills in the Classroom*, 77 NEB. L. REV. 132 (1998). A recent article looks at law teaching from a student's perspective: James B. Levy, *As a Last Resort, Ask the Students: What They Say Makes Someone an Effective Law Teacher*, 58 ME L. REV. 49 (2006) (surveying students on the characteristics that enable a law teacher to create a classroom atmosphere conducive to learning).

2   *See* MADELEINE SCHACHTER, THE LAW PROFESSOR'S HANDBOOK: A PRACTICAL GUIDE TO TEACHING LAW (2004) (offering useful and detailed advice on designing, administering, and teaching a law school course). *See also* PHILIP C. KISSAM, THE DISCIPLINE OF LAW SCHOOLS: THE MAKING OF MODERN LAWYERS (2003) (taking a sharply critical look at the routine practices and habits that are deeply embedded in law school teaching).

3   *See* WILLIAM M. SULLIVAN ET AL., CARNEGIE FOUNDATION FOR THE ADVANCEMENT OF TEACHING, EDUCATING LAWYERS: PREPARATION FOR THE PROFESSION OF LAW (2007) [hereinafter THE CARNEGIE REPORT].

4   *See, e.g.,* TEACHING THE LAW SCHOOL CURRICULUM (Steven Friedland & Gerald F. Hess eds., 2004); GERALD F. HESS & STEVEN FRIEDLAND, TECHNIQUES FOR TEACHING LAW (1999).

5   *See, e.g.,* GREGORY S. MUNRO, OUTCOMES ASSESSMENT FOR LAW SCHOOLS (2000).

6   ROY STUCKEY ET AL., CLINICAL LEGAL EDUCATION ASSOCIATION, BEST PRACTICES FOR LEGAL EDUCATION (2007) [hereinafter THE CLEA REPORT], *available at* http://www.cleaweb.org/resources/bp.html (last visited Apr. 8, 2009).

7   *See, e.g.,* Albany Law School, Best Practices for Legal Education blog, *available at* http://bestpracticeslegaled.albanylawblogs.org (last visited Jan. 5, 2009); Elon University School of Law, Center for Engaged Learning in the Law (CELL) blog, *available at* http://idd.elon.edu/blogs/law (last visited Jan. 5, 2009); Law School Innovations blog, *available at* http://lsi.typepad.com/lsi (last visited Jan. 5, 2009).

8   *See, e.g.,* Barbara Glesner Fines, University of Missouri-Kansas City School of Law, Teaching and Learning Law: Resources for Legal Education, *available at* http://www.law.umkc.edu/faculty/profiles/glesnerfines/bgf-edu.htm (last visited Jan. 5, 2009); Emory University School of Law, Center for Transactional Law and Practice, Transactional Training Resource Guide, *available at* http://www.law.emory.edu/programs-centers-clinics/transactional-law-program/trans-law-resources.html (last visited Jan. 5, 2009).

9   THE LAW TEACHER (Michael Hunter Schwartz & Gerald F. Hess eds.) (jointly published by Gonzaga University School of Law and Washburn University School of Law), *available at* http://washburnlaw.edu/faculty/schwartz-michael-institute/15-1lawteacher(2008).pdf.

10   In our view, the contributions of Kent Syverud, Susan Becker, and Douglas Whaley are especially valuable. *See* Kent D. Syverud, *Taking Students Seriously: A Guide for New Law Teachers*, 43 J. LEGAL EDUC. 247 (1993); Susan J. Becker, *Advice for the New Law Professor: A View from the Trenches*, 42 J. LEGAL EDUC. 432 (1992); Douglas J. Whaley, *Teaching Law: Advice for the New Professor*, 43 OHIO ST. L.J. 125 (1982).

11   SCHACHTER, *supra* note 2, comes closest to this aim. It is well worth consulting, but we have tried here to offer more detailed advice.

12　*See* THE WAR ROOM (Vidmark/Trimark Pictures 1994) (directed by D.A. Pennebaker & Chris Hegedus) (revealing the conscious effort in Bill Clinton's first presidential campaign to focus on a limited number of themes in order to convey those themes effectively). In the final days of the 2008 presidential election, campaign insiders attributed John McCain's imminent defeat to an abject *failure* of "message discipline." Tom Baldwin, *Pep Talk Is Drowned Out by Recriminations*, TIMES (London), Oct. 27, 2008, *available at* 2008 WLNR 20467302.

13　*See, e.g.,* HESS & FRIEDLAND, *supra* note 4 (offering a wealth of suggestions on specific classroom techniques).

14　We have written this book at a point in time when there is no longer any clear consensus on how the law should be taught. Though the traditional approach to classroom instruction is still widely practiced, eloquent voices are calling for change — THE CARNEGIE REPORT (*supra* note 3 at 14) and THE CLEA REPORT (*supra* note 6 at 8-9) both call for an increased focus on skills training, and THE CLEA REPORT (*supra* note 6 at 132-33) urges a reduced reliance on the Socratic dialogue and case method. Accordingly, this book offers suggestions on skills training and innovative classroom techniques, while providing abundant advice on improving the effectiveness of traditional classroom instruction. An excellent resource for innovations in law teaching is the website of the Legal Education at the Crossroads conference, held at the University of Washington School of Law on September 5-7, 2008, *available at* http://files.law.washington.edu/open/Crossroads_Conference/ (last visited Jan. 6, 2009).

15　For additional observations on the benefits of being "transparent," see *infra* § IV(D).

16　*See* Sophie M. Sparrow, *Describing the Ball: Improve Teaching by Using Rubrics — Explicit Grading Criteria*, 2004 MICH. ST. L. REV. 1, 6 (advocating greater transparency in law school grading standards through the implementation of "rubrics, or detailed written grading criteria, which describe both what students should learn and how they will be evaluated").

17　This statement is uttered by Andrew Shepherd, the title character in THE AMERICAN PRESIDENT (Columbia/Universal Pictures 1995) (directed by Rob Reiner).

18　*See supra* note 12.

19　It's OK to make an occasional observation that relates to a goal you rejected. And a mid-course correction may be necessary if your students seem to be drowning. But when you broach or pursue a discarded goal, you are burning up a scarce and precious commodity — classroom time. When it comes to budgeting that time, don't expect your students to absorb anything that you say only once.

20　For more on this point, see *infra* § VI(G).

21　It is no answer for a professor to say, "It's not my job to teach legal analysis. That's something my students should be learning in their legal writing class." It is *every* professor's job to teach legal analysis. By refusing to be bothered with it, a professor sends a message to her students that legal analysis is somehow inapplicable to her course and to her exam. It is precisely this effort to compartmentalize legal analysis, shunting it off as the sole responsibility of legal writing instructors, that leaves many students confused about what they are supposed to be learning in law school and what is expected of them on their exams.

22　Later in this book, we devote an entire section to problems and hypotheticals. *See infra* § VI(E).

23　Useful for this purpose are Aspen's "Crunchtime," "Inside," and "Essentials" series; West's "Nutshell" and "Concise Hornbook" series; the "Mastering" series from Carolina Academic Press; and the "Concepts and Insights" series from Foundation Press.

24　At this early stage, you may not grasp or retain the full significance of what you read in the hornbook anyway. It will become much more useful once classes have commenced and specific issues start popping up — when fielding questions from students or working through your day-to-day preparation for class.

25   Law review articles can be very helpful, but they do have their limitations as an aid to teaching. They are best at helping you to see the nuances of your subject and the major areas of contention within it. But bear in mind that most of what you'll learn from law reviews will be useful to you only as background. Unless your course is a very specialized one, or unless your objectives include a rather sophisticated level of analysis, you will traverse many pages in a law review article before finding something that can be brought directly into your classroom.

26   When looking for useful questions, illustrations, and hypotheticals, remember to consult the teacher's manuals of casebooks in your subject area. For a general discussion of teacher's manuals, see *infra* § III(B)(8). For a discussion of teacher's manuals as a "shadow source," see *infra* § III(A)(3).

27   When imposing an initial structure upon your teaching outline, you may find it useful to adopt the same order of presentation as that employed by the casebook from which you'll be teaching.

28   *See infra* § VI(G) (where we advocate taking notes, immediately after each class session, about what worked and what didn't work — so that you can benefit from these observations the next time you teach the course).

29   Jerome A. Barron, C. Thomas Dienes, Wayne McCormack & Martin H. Redish, Constitutional Law: Principles and Policy, Cases and Materials (7th ed. 2006) (LexisNexis).

30   Daniel A. Farber, William N. Eskridge, Jr. & Philip P. Frickey, Constitutional Law: Themes for the Constitution's Third Century (4th ed. 2009) (Thomson West).

31   The major legal publishers include Aspen, Thomson West, Foundation Press, LexisNexis, and Carolina Academic Press.

32   Hoping to influence your decision, the publishers will send you any teacher's manual that accompanies a given casebook. They will also send you a number of secondary sources, mainly hornbooks and treatises, in the hope that you'll select one of them as a required or recommended text. Normally they will not send commercial outlines — Emanuel, Gilbert, Sum & Substance — unless you specifically request them.

33   Switching to a different book is easier in some courses (e.g., Contracts or Constitutional Law) where there is common agreement about some or all of the classic or leading cases. Those cases will be in *all* the books.

34   Finding the right book is more art than science, and even some experienced teachers will admit that they don't have it completely figured out. The difficulty for a new teacher is that you've never used a casebook as a *teaching tool*, so you don't know exactly what to look for. But you did spend thousands of hours poring over casebooks as a student — and if there were any casebook characteristics that you found particularly helpful or unhelpful, you can use those recollections to inform your decision.

35   You might ask, for example, if any passages are particularly troublesome for students and, if so, how best to navigate them. You might also ask if there are any passages that your colleague does not assign as being redundant or straying too far afield.

36   One option, of course, was to adopt a conventional casebook and supplement it with problems and exercises of his own creation. But he wasn't confident that he could cook up an adequate supply of his own problems prior to the start of classes, or that he could maintain the quality of those exercises if he tried to craft them as the semester went along. While his long-range goal was to draft many such problems, he envisioned doing so over a period of years, not weeks — guided in large part by the experience of *teaching* Evidence to many students over several semesters. For now, at least, he wanted a text that shared his commitment to the problem approach.

37   Christopher B. Mueller & Laird C. Kirkpatrick, Evidence Under the Rules (6th ed. 2008) (Aspen).

38   This points up the danger of focusing on best-sellers. It can cause you to ignore new and innovative books that are just starting to attract attention. That danger is greater now than ever before — because the consensus over how and what to teach has broken down, prompting a host of new titles to enter the marketplace. One modern (and laudable) trend is to develop books that are more accessible to students.

39   Those notes can function as a type of "shadow source." For our discussion of shadow sources, see *supra* § III(A)(3).

40   *See supra* § III(B).

41   One of us succumbed to this temptation the first time he taught Constitutional Law. Among the available casebooks, the Barron & Dienes book (*supra* note 29) caught his eye — in part because it was then the only casebook that included *Miami Herald Publishing Company v. Tornillo*, 418 U.S. 241 (1974). The central question in the *Miami Herald* case — whether newspapers can be compelled by statute to provide a "right of reply" to candidates whom they criticize — was particularly interesting to him. That Barron & Dienes stood alone among the major casebooks as the only one to include *Miami Herald* was a factor that favorably impressed him — and it contributed to his adoption of that book. In retrospect, this was not a sound basis for making the decision. By placing far too much emphasis on a relatively minor detail, it could easily have led him astray. Fortunately, Barron & Dienes turned out to be a very good casebook. But it's a good casebook for reasons that have nothing to do with the myopic criteria he used in selecting it. In retrospect, the presence or absence of a single case should not be a factor in choosing a book. It's easy enough to supply a missing case by giving it to the students yourself or having them access it electronically.

42   *See infra* § III(B)(3).

43   *See infra* § III(B)(7).

44   You should select a book not because it is likely to entertain you, but because it is the best available teaching tool — the book that is most likely to promote your students' understanding. A close cousin of the professor who selects the book that he personally finds most stimulating is the professor who staves off boredom by deliberately *changing* books every two or three years. While such energy and commitment are admirable (and certainly preferable to the professor who never modifies or rethinks his course), changing books on a frequent basis is not beneficial to your students unless there are several books on the market having equal value *as teaching tools*. If one book is clearly paramount, your students deserve to read it. Each student only takes the course once; to subject her to an inferior teaching vehicle cannot be justified if the main purpose in selecting that book is to fend off the professor's boredom. There are other ways — incorporating new exercises, creating new hypotheticals, adding new illustrations of traditional doctrines — to stay fresh.

45   Jesse Dukeminier, James E. Krier, Gregory S. Alexander & Michael H. Schill, Property (6th ed. 2006) (Aspen).

46   Many law schools devote five or six semester hours to the Property course.

47   If you assign it, students *will* ask questions about it — and that means you'll have to spend time immersing yourself in material that you've already decided does not warrant coverage. Fending off an occasional question about note material is fully justified, whether in the interest of time or out of concern that delving into it will leave too many other students confused. But remember this about blowing off student questions: Do it too often and you will appear to lack knowledge of your subject. You may even create the impression that you harbor a general unwillingness to answer student questions.

48   If a point is worth making, it doesn't have to be in your casebook; you can always raise it your-self. And even if the point *is* contained in your casebook, there's no guarantee that your students will understand it. If the point is important, you need to spend *class time* to ensure that they grasp it.

49   *See infra* note 90 and accompanying text (stressing the need to "situate" the topic you're cover-ing in its larger doctrinal context).

50   Wrongly decided or minority-rule cases can be used to explore any number of issues — the com-peting policy concerns that produced a split in the case law; factual variations that may have prompted divergent outcomes; judicial myopia in the stubborn adherence to outdated precedent; or errors of judicial analysis that betray a flawed understanding of the governing doctrine.

51   Another option is to borrow problems from other books.

52   *See supra* note 36.

53   *See supra* § III(B)(3).

54   While bearing these concerns in mind, don't let us discourage you from supplementing a case-book with problems or exercises of your own creation. Such a project is by no means doomed to failure. One of us has successfully integrated nearly 100 problems into his First Amendment course, while using a casebook that is not problem-oriented: Geoffrey R. Stone, Louis M. Seidman, Cass R. Sunstein, Mark V. Tushnet & Pamela S. Karlan, The First Amendment (3d ed. 2008) (Aspen) [hereinafter Stone Seidman]. He uses Stone Seidman to immerse his students in a particular First Amendment topic (e.g., prior restraint) and then tests their under-standing by asking them to analyze certain fact patterns that are based on lower-court opinions. Far from conflicting, the casebook and the problems actually complement one another in con-tributing to the students' understanding.

55   Dobbs, for example, is a classic short-case book. Dan B. Dobbs & Paul T. Hayden, Torts and Compensation — Personal Accountability and Social Responsibility for Injury (6th ed. 2009) (Thomson West). Barnett, on the other hand, exemplifies the long-case tradi-tion. Randy E. Barnett, Contracts: Cases and Doctrine (4th ed. 2008) (Aspen). An echo of the long-case/short-case dichotomy may be found in books that employ a problem approach. Crandall and Whaley, for example, feature problems that are short and compact. Thomas D. Crandall & Douglas J. Whaley, Cases, Problems, and Materials on Contracts (5th ed. 2008) (Aspen). Knapp and Crystal utilize problems that are much longer. Charles L. Knapp, Nathan M. Crystal & Harry G. Prince, Problems in Contract Law: Cases and Materi-als (6th ed. 2007) (Aspen).

56   One disadvantage of being a long-case professor is that it's harder to figure out the pacing of your assignments, because each case can be the occasion for an extended class discussion on a variety of points, and it can be difficult to predict or control how long that discussion will take.

57   *See supra* § III(A)(3).

58   *See supra* §§ II(A) & II(B).

59   *See, e.g.,* Barnett, *supra* note 55.

60   *See supra* § III(B)(4).

61   Dukeminier, *supra* note 45.

62   It might well take a toll on you, too, since you'll have to prepare to teach all those pages.

63   These pacing problems can be especially acute if a short-case teacher adopts a long-case book. For our discussion of long-case versus short-case teachers, see *supra* § III(B)(6).

64   *See supra* § III(B)(3).

65   In answering these questions, it is perfectly appropriate to consult a BARBRI outline or any of the widely used commercial outlines to identify the minimum conventional coverage of a subject.

66   *See supra* § II(B).

67   For advice on how many pages to assign per class session, see *supra* § III(C)(1)(a).

68   As you scan the topics that comprise your course in search of likely candidates for compression, bear one thing in mind — sometimes *expanding* the topic or having it do double duty may be preferable to compressing it. An example is the Dormant Commerce Clause. It's a topic that inspires scant interest in students and professors alike and might readily be targeted for compression. But one of us uses the Dormant Commerce Clause to teach the basic distinction between discriminatory intent and discriminatory effect — a topic that is normally covered in the politically charged context of race discrimination. He believes that students gain a clearer understanding of that important distinction when they encounter it first in the less emotional realm of economic regulations. Thus, the classroom time that he spends on the Dormant Commerce Clause — time he *used to* begrudge — now serves to accomplish multiple objectives.

69   See *supra* note 21 and *infra* § IV(I) on teaching legal analysis.

70   *See supra* § III(B)(4).

71   This does not mean that every foundational concept must be *mastered* before proceeding. If students would not be ready to tackle such a concept at the semester's outset, simply *introduce* the concept, proceed to less challenging topics, and then circle back to it later in your course. In Torts the foundational concept of *duty* exemplifies this problem. The concept of duty is so important in Torts that students should be exposed to it early on, but they need not master it before learning anything else. After introducing the concept, you might proceed to the intentional torts, structuring your course so that duty is covered later in the semester. Another way of dealing with a foundational concept is to identify it for your students and then, before proceeding onward, ask them to make an *assumption* about it. In Constitutional Law, for example, a major question blocks the roadway at the very start of the course: the legitimacy of judicial review. As we advise below (*infra* § III(C)(1)(d)), this question is best covered *after* the students have seen some memorable examples of the critical role that judicial review has played in our system of checks and balances. Thus, at the very start of the course, you can simply ask them to *assume* its legitimacy. Another example of this technique comes from the Contracts course. The Statute of Frauds plays an important role in contract law, but delving into it early in the first semester will leave your students needlessly confused. Go ahead and broach the idea that some contracts must be in writing to be enforceable. Ask them to *assume* for now that contracts don't have to be in writing, and assure them that you'll refine that idea later in the semester.

72   Under such an approach, you would introduce Rule 8 and Rule 38 at the same time. Though these provisions are set forth in very different sections of the Civil Rules, and though they might not seem related at first glance, they are both critically important at the same stage of a lawsuit — when the plaintiff is drafting the complaint. Rule 8(a) identifies the key components that comprise a complaint, while Rule 38(b) permits a jury demand to be set forth in a party's initial pleading. This is an example of how seemingly disparate topics can be linked together in your syllabus due to their logical connection — and how such linkage can benefit your students by getting them to see a connection that might otherwise have escaped their attention.

73   For suggestions on how to begin your course, see *infra* § V(B). One word of caution here: Don't get sucked into spending *too* much time on introductory material. Instead of spending two or three weeks, keep it short. Then, five weeks into the semester, *come back* to those introductory themes and your students will get more out of them. Once you spend that second or third week, it's gone — and you may be sorry in Week 13 when you're trying not to rush the end of your course.

74   The offer and acceptance rules are not necessarily the ideal starting point either. Offer is a tricky concept; it is not neatly reducible to elements, and often proves vexing to first-year students. Unlike Torts, for example, some courses have no ideal starting point.

75   *See supra* notes 15-16 and accompanying text; *see infra* § IV(D).

76   *See infra* note 90 and accompanying text.

77   5 U.S. (1 Cranch) 137 (1803).

78   14 U.S. (1 Wheat.) 304 (1816) (upholding power of U.S. Supreme Court to review decisions of the highest state courts that rest upon the interpretation of federal law).

79   Paco Underhill, Why We Buy: The Science of Shopping 62 (1999).

80   Erwin Chemerinsky, Constitutional Law 11-24 (3d ed. 2009) (Aspen).

81   One of us tells his students that it's like soccer — the official time is kept on the field by the referee.

82   It also presents the opposite problem: the danger that you will "*under*-assign" for a given class and run out of material with many minutes left on the clock. This problem is less likely to occur. Normally it takes *longer* to cover the material than you think it will, and this is particularly true if you are working through a problem in class. But on the off chance that you do run out of assigned material and you don't want to let your students out early, you should always have some additional material "in your hip pocket." In the early weeks of a course, particularly in the first-year courses, this might be an icebreaker (e.g., having each student give their name, their undergraduate school, and their favorite course in college). It might also be an extended discussion of policy arguments that run through the course, or a review problem, or an illustrative story from practice, or a recent news item. If it is truly "additional" material, you may never use it. If it's important enough to include in the course no matter what, you will get to a point where you consistently cover it — and then you'll have to replace it in your mind with another assignment in reserve.

83   *See infra* § VII(B).

84   This topic has triggered a small avalanche of discussion. Here are two recent articles that are well worth reading: Jana R. McCreary, *The Laptop-Free Zone*, 49 Val. U. L. Rev. ___ (2009), *available at* SSRN: http://ssrn.com/abstract=1280929 (Oct. 8, 2008) (last visited Apr. 8, 2009); Kevin Yamamoto, *Banning Laptops in the Classroom: Is It Worth the Hassles?*, 57 J. Legal Educ. 477 (2007).

85   *See supra* notes 15-16 and accompanying text; *see infra* § IV(D).

86   *See infra* § IV(E).

87   Bearing in mind your duty to behave in a professional manner (*see supra* § IV(A)), you should steer clear of using humor on a host of subjects. We needn't recite them all, but human sexuality, race, and religion top the list. The most important thing to remember is this: Never make fun of your students. For them, the law school experience is humbling enough. When a professor tries to be funny, *self-deprecating* humor is the safest path.

88   This is why it is so important for the professor to stress that memorizing cases is not an end in itself; that it is pointless to internalize each case as if it could be invoked, like some magic incantation, on the exam; that, instead, cases are simply hypotheticals that happen to have happened, and should therefore be regarded mainly as vehicles for understanding the application of facts to law.

89   *See infra* note 136 and accompanying text.

90   Henceforth we'll refer to this technique in shorthand fashion as "situating" the topic or material.

91   A fine article on creating a beneficial classroom atmosphere is: Gerald F. Hess, *Heads and Hearts: The Teaching and Learning Environment in Law School*, 52 J. LEGAL EDUC. 75 (2002).

92   The best way to learn the names of your students is to convert their individual photographs into a set of flash cards, with their faces on one side and their names on the other. It's a simple matter to review the cards, face by face, challenging yourself to recall each corresponding name.

93   Even if you decide not to use your seating chart as an attendance sheet, it's still a good idea to make multiple photocopies of it, because the one you need for the podium tends to disappear two minutes before the start of class.

94   By utilizing the enrollment roster, your assistant can create all of the name placards before the first day of class. Thus, you can already be calling on students by name even *before* you've created a seating chart — if, like both of us, you announce on the first day of class that your seating chart will be based on the seats they occupy on the second day of class.

95   If you rely solely upon volunteers, you may unwittingly create an atmosphere in which the male students will dominate class discussions. Men tend to be much more talkative than women in the classroom — and if the instructor is male and the majority of students are male, the resulting imbalance will be severe, with the male students speaking two and a half times longer than their female peers. Catherine G. Krupnick, *Women and Men in the Classroom: Inequality and Its Remedies*, http://isites.harvard.edu/fs/html/icb.topic58474/krupnick.html, Online Document, Harvard University, Derek Bok Center for Teaching and Learning (1985) (last visited Apr. 8, 2009).

96   Remote personal response systems, popularly known as "clickers," look like simplified TV remote control units — and they are used by students to transmit immediate responses to multiple choice questions posed by their teacher. The system operates with infrared or radio frequency technology. A small, portable receiving station is placed at the front of the classroom to collect and record student responses. Each clicker can be registered to a student (or not, depending on the teacher's preference) and generates a unique, identifiable signal. *See* Educause Learning Initiative, *7 Things You Should Know About Clickers*, http://connect.educause.edu/Library/ELI/7ThingsYouShouldKnowAbout/39379 (last visited Apr. 4, 2009). Here is an example of how clickers can be used. *See id.* When students arrive in the classroom, they pull their clickers out of their backpacks in preparation for the start of class. The teacher begins her presentation by reviewing an important concept that she covered in the previous class session. She then asks the students to answer a multiple choice question designed to gauge how well they understand the concept she just reviewed. The students take their clickers in hand. Displaying the question on an overhead projector, she tells the students that they have 90 seconds in which to answer. They are confronted with five different choices — (a), (b), (c), (d), and (e) — and their clickers are equipped with five corresponding buttons. As the students transmit their answers, a running tally of student responses is projected on the screen. When the 90 seconds have elapsed, the teacher displays a bar chart of the poll results. It is immediately apparent that the students are confused; their responses are evenly split across all five options. Now the students' curiosity is aroused; they want to know which answer is correct. At this point, the teacher can ask them to pair up and convince their partner that their response is correct. After a few minutes of boisterous discussion, the teacher polls them again. The responses are better but not perfect. Now she really has their attention — she can explain the concept and highlight the source of the confusion. *See generally* DOUGLAS DUNCAN, CLICKERS IN THE CLASSROOM: HOW TO ENHANCE SCIENCE TEACHING USING CLASSROOM RESPONSE SYSTEMS (2005) (offering detailed guidance on the use of this technology).

97   TWEN® is an acronym for The West Education Network, an online service furnished by Westlaw that provides law professors with Web-based course management tools. TWEN is available on the

Web at http://www.lawschool.westlaw.com. Using TWEN, professors can create online courses, post course materials, distribute assignments, take attendance, administer online quizzes, and obtain immediate feedback on specific questions by conducting an "InstaPoll" in which students register their reaction while logged in during class. We discuss TWEN below in section VII(B), "Creating a Web Page for Your Class."

98 Well worth considering are two methods that have each gained wider acceptance over the past decade — (1) breaking students into small "buzz groups," comprised of six or fewer people, and directing them to discuss particular issues or problems for short spans of time, THE CLEA REPORT, *supra* note 6, at 132; and (2) using classroom "clickers," *supra* note 96, to conduct live polls of the entire class in response to multiple choice questions posed at various points throughout the session.

99 This is true even though random interrogation is *designed* to compel student preparedness through the threat of public embarrassment. That threat loses its power over time. Eventually, it isn't strong enough to overcome any number of countervailing forces in a student's life — e.g., the demands and deadlines imposed by an employer; law review or moot court obligations; a decreasing fear of law professors; exhaustion; or good old-fashioned laziness. Thus, unpreparedness is a fact of life under the random interrogation approach. If you don't *go looking for it* (i.e., if you don't randomly probe twenty students per day), you won't find so much of it. This is one of the attractions of the expert panel approach. It doesn't scour the classroom *in search* of unpreparedness. It strikes a bargain with unpreparedness — giving the student advance warning of her performance and thereby guaranteeing that she'll be ready.

100 *See supra* § IV(F)(1).

101 *See supra* § III(C)(2).

102 Nor do we advocate tantrums of a less-than-volcanic magnitude. Sighing, snorting, or other manifestations of disdain — even if they fall short of Krakatoan proportions — are not a productive response to unpreparedness. You can insist upon standards, of course. But your overriding tone should be empathetic, supportive, enthusiastic, and *patient*. We are not patient people in real life, but each of us plays the *role* of a patient person in the classroom.

103 THE CLEA REPORT, *supra* note 6 at 132, specifically recommends the use of such "buzz groups."

104 You might also assign review problems in advance of class; when the students arrive, break into small groups and ask them to improve their answers through collaboration.

105 *See infra* § VI(B).

106 With any courtroom simulation or skills exercise, you are accomplishing several useful objectives. You are: (1) stimulating interest, which can lead to (2) better doctrinal understanding and performance; and, by teaching the students how to perform as courtroom lawyers, you are (3) introducing and modeling professionalism. (Such exercises don't have to be elaborate or time-consuming to accomplish these goals.) Seen in this light, simulations and experiential learning do not conflict with doctrinal understanding; they support it. *See* Deborah Maranville, *Infusing Passion and Context into the Traditional Law Curriculum through Experiential Learning*, 51 J. LEGAL EDUC. 51 (2001).

107 FED. R. CIV. P. 12(b)(2) (motion to dismiss for lack of personal jurisdiction).

108 FED. R. EVID. 612.

109 If you can find the time to give every single student at least one of these direct examination exercises, then your class will begin thinking and talking about evidence in terms of the question-and-answer format by which it comes in at trial. In other words, they will start to picture

evidentiary issues not as free-floating abstractions but in the concrete context of the courtroom — as the product of direct and cross-examination, of testimony and exhibits.

110   To a certain extent, the reaction of students to given topics is predictable. Over time a professor will identify specific areas that are likely to cause confusion, year after year and even with the best of fine-tuning. (In Evidence, for example, the hearsay rule is inevitably a stumbling block for even the most gifted students, no matter how inventive the presentation.) This creates a challenge for you as you gain more experience. You'll want to teach each new class as a group of unique individuals, while at the same time recognizing patterns that recur year after year.

111   *See supra* note 97.

112   *See supra* note 96.

113   This same theme can apply to other courses — Torts and Property suggest themselves readily. But the idea of formalism, and the battles around that concept, are obviously central in the unfolding of contract doctrines.

114   168 So. 196 (Ala. Ct. App. 1935).

115   *See supra* § IV(E).

116   George Burns, American comedian and actor (1896-1996). Encarta, *Quotations*, http://encarta. msn.com/quote_561553428/Acting_and_Actors_The_secret_of_acting_is_sincerity_If_you_.html (last visited Apr. 6, 2009).

117   As we've already observed, you may want to pass around the seating chart on the *second* day, having alerted your students on the first day. *See supra* § IV(F)(1).

118   *See infra* § V(B)(3).

119   Several years after graduating from law school, a former student stopped one of us on the street and singled out the Goodyear Blimp Overview as the single most helpful method she had encountered as a law student. This is not to say that students normally wait until after graduation to praise the method. They often mention it favorably in their semester-end course evaluations.

120   *See infra* § V(B)(2).

121   *See infra* § V(B)(1).

122   Depending on the classroom dynamic, you may have difficulty getting students to volunteer their individual reactions while sitting in a large audience. If this happens, simply break them up into smaller groups and explain that each group will be called upon to report its reactions in fifteen or twenty minutes. In the relative security of a small group, students will likely feel less inhibited.

123   *See* Treesh v. Taft, 122 F. Supp. 2d 881 (S.D. Ohio 2000).

124   *See* Alan Johnson, *Last Words Back in Ohio's Execution Ritual*, Columbus Dispatch, Apr. 10, 2001, *available at* http://www.dispatch.com/news/news01/apr01/655029.html.

125   *See* Kevin Francis O'Neill, *Muzzling Death Row Inmates: Applying the First Amendment to Regulations That Restrict a Condemned Prisoner's Last Words*, 33 Ariz. St. L.J. 1159 (2001).

126   *See* Kevin Francis O'Neill, *A First Amendment Compass: Navigating the Speech Clause with a Five-Step Analytical Framework*, 29 Sw. U. L. Rev. 223, 291-96 (2000) (discussing the restricted environment cases).

127   *See id.* at 270-77 (discussing prior restraint).

128   *See id.* at 278-82 (discussing overbreadth).

129   *See id.* at 234-43 (comparing content-based restrictions with time/place/manner regulations).

130 Other lines of First Amendment precedent embedded in this fact pattern include: the general prohibition against "unfettered discretion" in regulating speech; the importance of focusing on the government's *purpose* in adopting a speech restriction; resort to the public forum doctrine when a speaker tries to use government property as the platform for her speech; and the lesser protection afforded certain "low-level" categories of speech, like profanity, obscenity, and fighting words.

131 A similar objective can be achieved through the use of an introductory case that features vivid or amusing facts, or with a matched set of cases bearing similar facts but divergent outcomes. In the vivid-or-amusing-facts category are two cases that have often been used to kick off the courses in Contracts and Property: Lucy v. Zehmer, 84 S.E.2d 516 (Va. 1954) (enforcing $50,000 contract to sell a farm, negotiated in a restaurant while the two parties were drinking heavily, even though the seller believed that the buyer's offer had been made in jest and the parties wrote their agreement on the back of a restaurant check); Pierson v. Post, 3 Cai. R. 175 (N.Y. Sup. Ct. 1805) (riding on horseback and accompanied by his hounds, plaintiff was closely pursuing a fox when defendant intercepted and killed the fox and then carried it away; court holds that plaintiff never acquired a property interest in the fox). One point to keep in mind, regarding any introductory cases employed in first-year or major second-year courses, is that you must go slow, because the approach and the terminology are apt to be new and confusing. Any paragraph of any case examined on the first day of class can probably be parsed to the point of consuming an entire class session.

132 *See* Grant Gilmore, The Death of Contract 19-21 (1974).

133 *Id.* at 21.

134 How much detail should you provide? A good rule of thumb is to give your students enough information to afford a basic grasp of the doctrine, without piling on so many finer points as to make it seem unfathomable.

135 In this way, the Goodyear Blimp Overview enhances your ability to "situate the material" as you move through the course. *See supra* note 90 and accompanying text (describing the technique of "situating the material" for your students). You can begin and end every class session by tying the day's topic back to the Goodyear Blimp Overview, specifying where the topic fits within the larger doctrinal outline of your course.

136 The Paper Chase (Twentieth Century Fox Film Corp. 1973) (directed by James Bridges). Based on the 1970 novel by John Jay Osborn, Jr., *The Paper Chase* tells the story of Hart, a first-year student at Harvard Law School, and his experiences with a brilliant but demanding Contracts professor, Charles W. Kingsfield, Jr. (memorably played by John Houseman).

137 *See supra* § IV(D).

138 By "Socratic," we mean Kingsfield-style interrogation, where the professor *only* asks questions and provides no answers. *See supra* note 89 and accompanying text.

139 We touch briefly upon entry questions at an earlier point in this article — in the paragraph that culminates in footnote 105.

140 Tightly scripting the opening questions in a law school classroom was partly inspired by a National Football League precedent. *See* David Harris, The Genius: How Bill Walsh Reinvented Football and Created an NFL Dynasty 101 (2008) (describing the practice, pioneered by coach Bill Walsh, of scripting the first twenty plays to be run by a football team at the start of a game). For an explanation of how to prepare for class using a highly scripted and detailed format (as well as other general advice on teaching), see Donald H. Zeigler, How I Teach (2008) (New York: Tribeca Square Press).

141 There is a point worth making here that does not specifically pertain to entry questions but does very much relate to this section's topic — controlling the flow of class discussion when analyzing

a judicial decision. When orchestrating the class discussion of a case, you will sometimes be faced with the following question: Should you discuss the issues and analysis presented by the case in the very same sequence set out in the court's opinion, or should you rearrange them in ways that might better suit your pedagogical purposes? As we all know, judges don't always present their ideas in the most logical order. Judicial opinions can be repetitive, central issues can be left to the end, and threshold questions can appear in the middle. But your students, particularly early in their law school careers (and often influenced by the emphasis at some schools on a rather mechanical notion of case briefing), will likely have "prepped" the cases as written. Deviating from that sequence in class may cause confusion, and induce frantic flipping of pages as students try to figure out where you are in the case. Over the course of a semester, as your students become more accustomed to your style of legal analysis, it may be easier for you to rearrange the sequence of an opinion to suit your purposes. You may even find that doing it early in the term sends a strong message of how good, logical, step-by-step analysis should be performed. The key is to recognize the likely inclination of your students to follow the order set out in the opinion. Mindful of that, you can make a better and more conscious decision on whether to deviate.

142   *See infra* § VI(F)(2).

143   *See supra* text culminating in footnote 105.

144   You might begin with a problem that poses the same issue as the assigned case but is factually quite different from it. You could start with the problem and then move to the case, checking to see if their factual differences prevent the students from recognizing that they have an issue in common. Or you might begin with an "ought" question — "Ought the plaintiff to recover here?" — and then work back to the governing rule and the fairness of that rule. Or you might begin by proposing a factual variation on the assigned case and then working back to the facts as they actually happened. Thus, you might say: "In the instant case, X happened; but what if, instead, the Y didn't Z?" This forces the student to identify which fact is in play, working back to the governing rule and then forward to the rule's application in the actual case, all with a view toward determining whether the change in facts requires a change in outcome.

145   *See* George F. Will, Men at Work: The Craft of Baseball 205 (1990) (describing the batting style of Tony Gwynn, Hall of Fame outfielder for the San Diego Padres, as "Wait-wait-wait and then quick-quick-quick.").

146   This is just friendly advice to young professors on a very specific teaching technique. It's *micro*-level advice. But there are some *macro*-level lessons to be learned here. Your reaction to the tension we describe — between exerting control and letting go — will reveal your preferences on the larger question of classroom management. And the more that you are comfortable letting go, the greater is the likelihood that you'll embrace alternative teaching methods (like breaking the class into small groups, as suggested by Hess & Friedland, *supra* note 4) that involve a loss of control.

147   *See supra* § IV(A).

148   *See supra* § III(A)(1).

149   Some students are deeply troubled by any question or any answer that they do not immediately understand. But their anxiety vanishes upon finding that they won't be responsible for that material on your exam.

150   *See* Restatement (Second) of Contracts § 90(1) (1981).

151   Three such cases can be found in Randy Barnett's casebook on Contracts. *See* Barnett, *supra* note 55, at 772-91 (featuring Blatt v. University of Southern California, 85 Cal. Rptr. 601 (Cal. Ct. App. 1970); Spooner v. Reserve Life Insurance Co., 287 P.2d 735 (Wash. 1955); Ypsilanti v. General Motors, 506 N.W.2d 556 (Mich. Ct. App. 1993)).

152 Presenting problems at the end of a chapter is an effective way to sum up and review everything you covered in that chapter. But problems can also be useful at the *beginning* of a chapter
when first exposing your students to a dense rule (i.e., a complex doctrine, cause of action,
or defense). Such rules can be baffling to students if viewed in isolation, without any factual
context. The purpose of an *introductory* problem is to give your students a concrete example of
the situation that the rule is meant to govern. One example of a dense rule is the cause of action
for fraudulent misrepresentation. It is comprised of the following elements: (1) An intentional
misrepresentation of fact (2) that is material and (3) intended (*"scienter"*) to induce and (4) does
induce reasonable reliance by the plaintiff (5) proximately causing (6) pecuniary harm to the
plaintiff. *See* Restatement (Second) of Torts § 525 (1977). This is a lot to digest — and your
students will have difficulty grasping the function and requirements of each element until they
gain a big-picture sense of the factual circumstances that constitute fraud. Thus, an effective way
to *begin* their study of fraud is to present them with a concrete fact pattern that satisfies each
of the requisite elements — or, better yet, two versions of the same basic fact pattern, in which
one satisfies and the other fails to satisfy all the elements. Use the problem simply to give your
students some practice identifying facts that speak to each element, with a view toward determining whether all the elements are satisfied. With this exercise behind them, the students are
now ready to read cases and commence a detailed study of each element.

153 *See supra* notes 36 & 52 and accompanying text.

154 *See, e.g.,* Mueller & Kirkpatrick, *supra* note 37 (featuring evidence problems); Crandall &
Whaley, *supra* note 55 (featuring contracts problems); Knapp & Crystal, *supra* note 55 (featuring contracts problems).

155 *See, e.g.,* Joseph W. Glannon, Civil Procedure: Examples & Explanations (6th ed. 2008)
(Aspen); Brian Blum, Contracts: Examples & Explanations (4th ed. 2007) (Aspen); Ar-
thur Best, Evidence: Examples & Explanations (6th ed. 2007) (Aspen). Additional subjects
in this series include Constitutional Law, Copyright, Corporations, Criminal Law, Criminal Procedure, Family Law, Federal Courts, Property, Remedies, Sales, Secured Transactions, Securities
Regulation, Torts, and Wills, Trusts, and Estates.

156 CALI is a non-profit consortium of law schools that develops computer-mediated legal instruction. Its website may be found at: http://www2.cali.org/. The CALI "Library of Lessons" is a
collection of over 600 interactive, computer-based lessons covering 32 different subject areas in
the law. These lessons are written by law faculty and librarians. The format varies depending
upon the author's educational objective. Some authors use the setting of a simulated trial that
pauses periodically for questions directed to the student, who plays the role of a lawyer or the
judge. Other authors create a fact pattern that serves as the basis for questions that require the
student to identify relevant issues and apply recently learned concepts.

157 We are not saying that students or professors should always proceed in this sequence when
performing legal analysis. Far from it. Our recommended approach to legal analysis — moving
element by element through the pending claims and defenses — is set forth emphatically enough
throughout this book. What we are saying here is that judicial opinions are traditionally comprised of the foregoing *segments* (just one of those segments being the analysis section), and that
students must be trained to recognize those segments, to understand the different function that
each segment performs, and to discern at any point in a given opinion which segment they are
reading. Without this training, students will have difficulty navigating an opinion and extracting
pertinent information from it. To put it simply, if we ask them to state the holding of the case,
we should not find them wandering around helplessly in the procedural posture. This training is
different from, and is best performed as a prelude to, instructing students how to perform legal
analysis. Dissecting the legal analysis *segment* of an opinion is the next step in that transition;
it's described in the text immediately below this note. Once you have performed the rudimentary
"dissection" exercises described in this section, you'll proceed to an activity that consumes a
great deal of time in law school classrooms: teaching legal analysis through a careful study of

the methods employed in judicial decisions. When scrutinizing a judge's analytical performance, professors are faced with a three-way choice. (1) You can follow the judge step by step, making no effort to repackage or deviate from the sequence of his observations. (Students are usually more comfortable proceeding in this fashion — but some casebooks feature judicial opinions that follow a downright illogical sequence, tempting the professor to impose a different order. *See supra* note 141.) (2) At the other extreme, you could disregard the judge's analytical steps, lay out the elements of the plaintiff's cause of action, and get your students to pull facts out of the opinion to see whether the elements are satisfied. (3) In the middle ground between the first two approaches, you could retrace the judge's steps, taking his ideas out of the opinion in the same sequence in which they appeared, and *plug them into* the elements. For a discussion of how reversing the traditional sequence of sections in a case brief can enhance student understanding of the case itself and of element-based analysis, see Hillary Burgess, *Beginners Brief Best By Briefing Backward (Sometimes)*, TEACHING METHODS NEWSLETTER (Association of American Law Schools, Washington, D.C.), Winter 2008, at 7, *available at* http://lawprofessors. typepad.com/academic_support/ (last visited Apr. 7, 2009).

158 105 S.W. 777 (Mo. Ct. App. 1907). Once again, this case can be found in the Contracts casebook by Randy Barnett. *See* BARNETT, *supra* note 55, at 290-94.

159 Our approach may invite some comparisons to "I-R-A-C," the well-known four-step approach to legal analysis (Issue-Rule-Application-Conclusion) that is taught at many law schools. Our approach is not a repudiation of I-R-A-C but rather a refinement of it. Our whole focus is on improving student performance of the Rule and Application steps. To help them achieve a truly fact-sensitive application, we believe that students must be given detailed advice on how to set up the governing rule, not just reducing it to elements but giving those elements sharper definition by incorporating their finer points from the caselaw. By breaking down the rule into very specific, sharply defined requirements, we make it easier for students to sift the facts and produce a nuanced application.

160 *See supra* § VI(E).

161 RESTATEMENT (SECOND) OF CONTRACTS § 90(1) (1981).

162 We want to stress that this exhortation — to break down the controlling law into elements — is not confined to causes of action. A mistaken assumption along those lines would be perfectly understandable because we have so far offered only two illustrations of elements (*see supra* notes 150-52 and accompanying text), and both of them (promissory estoppel and fraud) are causes of action. But any rule, any legal doctrine may be profitably reduced to elements, and this includes *defenses*. A good example may be found in the realm of contract law: the *impracticability of performance* defense. It is defined as follows:

> Where, after a contract is made, a party's performance is made impracticable without his fault by the occurrence of an event the non-occurrence of which was a basic assumption on which the contract was made, his duty to render that performance is discharged, unless the language or the circumstances indicate the contrary.

RESTATEMENT (SECOND) OF CONTRACTS § 261 (1981). First-year students will hardly find it easy to plug their facts into this dense mass of verbiage. The only sensible way to deal with this language is to break it down into elements: (1) A *supervening event* (after contract formation); (2) whose *non-occurrence* was a *basic assumption* upon which the contract was made; (3) that makes performance as agreed *impracticable* (i.e., that makes the promisor's performance *overwhelmingly burdensome*); (4) through *no fault* of the party seeking to be excused; and (5) neither the contract language nor the surrounding circumstances indicate that such party *assumed the risk* of the supervening event. Broken up into these smaller, more manageable pieces, the requirements of this rule are easier to see — making it easier to identify the facts that speak to them.

163 *See supra* text accompanying note 150.

164 *See supra* text accompanying note 151.

165 *See* BARNETT, *supra* note 55, at 772-91.

166 It may be useful to point out to your students that once a rule or an element has been intro-duced by a given case in the book, the next case will likely provide a new interpretation or limitation or refinement of the rule or element that was featured in the first case. With each new case, the student should be asking herself, "As to the pertinent rule or element, what does this case *add* to the knowledge I've already gleaned from the cases leading up to it?" Each new case in a given section can be used for yet another fruitful purpose. Students should take the facts from that case and use them as a hypothetical to *practice* the application of the rule, employing all of the glosses and refinements of the rule that have been learned up to that point.

167 This will help students to see that policy arguments recur and fit patterns, though obviously the strength of a given argument will vary among situations, just as some facts more clearly fit the black-letter rules than others.

168 Trial lawyers break their claims and defenses into elements so that they can monitor more care-fully their burden of proof — their duty to introduce evidence supporting each and every one of those elements. If they did not think of their cases in terms of elements, it would be much easier to overlook some aspect of their burden of proof, and that would leave them vulnerable to a directed verdict. *See* FED. R. CIV. P. 50(a). Well before any trial, a plaintiff's demonstrated inability to establish one element of her claim will expose her to summary judgment. *See* FED. R. CIV. P. 56(b). In criminal cases, the prosecutor must always be keenly aware of the elements that comprise the alleged crime, because she bears the burden of proving each of them beyond a reasonable doubt.

169 *See supra* § V(A)(2) (propounding the "unified field theory" of legal analysis).

170 An excellent new book that offers suggestions for incorporating technology into law school teaching is DAVID I. C. THOMSON, LAW SCHOOL 2.0: LEGAL EDUCATION FOR A DIGITAL AGE (2009) (LexisNexis).

171 Ellen Freedman & Donald J. Martin, *New Tricks: Learning to Use Courtroom Presentation Tools*, 23 PA. LAW. 28, 28 (Sept./Oct. 2001) ("Studies have consistently shown that visually reinforced information is easier to understand and remember and is in fact up to 650 times more effective than oral [presentation] alone.").

172 These drawbacks are not insurmountable. It is true that a PowerPoint presentation consists of slides that are placed in a particular sequence and that it is not feasible to edit that sequence in front of an audience. But manipulating the sequence of your slides is extremely easy and can be accomplished (during a break) in a matter of minutes. Moreover, if you need to jump *out* of sequence — because you've been asked to address a topic that is covered by some distant slides — it *is* possible (with an audience watching) to flip rapidly through your slides, forward or backward, to reach the desired passage. As for spontaneity, PowerPoint cannot rival the blackboard in readiness to address a new, unanticipated topic. But a PowerPoint presentation is not the irretrievable, unalterable chain reaction that some professors make it out to be. Once you become familiar with the program, you can jump out of the presentation mode while your audience watches and, in less than a minute, create a brand new slide that covers the new topic. Typing up the words in your new slide will not be substantially more time-consuming or disrup-tive than writing those words on the blackboard.

173 To visit the United States District Court for the Northern District of Ohio, for example, you would go to http://www.ohnd.uscourts.gov/ (last visited Apr. 8, 2009), and then click on "Judges." Each judge has his or her own Web page, where you can view their "Standing Orders."

174 To visit the website of YesVideo, Inc., go to http://www.yeslawdvd.com/ (offering product information on "Yeslaw Synchronized Legal Deposition Videos on DVD and CD") (last visited Apr. 8, 2009).

175 *See* MUELLER & KIRKPATRICK, *supra* note 37.

176 George Fisher's Evidence casebook for Foundation Press is supplemented by a VHS tape containing many film clips that are illustrative of various evidence rules. *See* GEORGE FISHER, EVIDENCE (2d ed. 2008) (Foundation Press).

177 Paul Wangerin, *Technology in the Service of Tradition: Electronic Lectures and Live-Class Teaching*, 53 J. LEGAL EDUC. 213 (2003) (observing that law students need to digest an abundance of background information on any new doctrine before they can apply it in performing legal analysis, and explaining how technology can be much more effective in conveying that background than straight lecture).

178 Robert E. Oliphant, *Using "Hi-Tech" Tools in a Traditional Classroom Environment: A Two-Semester Experiment*, 9 RICH. J.L. & TECH. 5 (Winter 2002-2003) (describing the author's extensive use of videotapes, PowerPoint, and CD-ROMs in the classroom when teaching first-year law students).

179 *See* http://www.uscourts.gov/images/CircuitMap.pdf (last visited Apr. 8, 2009).

180 *See supra* note 97.

181 Blackboard® is an online service that supplies professors with Web-based course management tools. It's available on the Web at: http://www.blackboard.com (last visited Apr. 8, 2009).

182 Contribute® is a software program created by Adobe Systems Inc. that makes it easy to edit or update existing websites or blogs, without having to learn HTML. For more information, go to: http://www.adobe.com/products/contribute/ (last visited Apr. 8, 2009).

183 No matter what subject you teach, there will be relevant stories from time to time in the newspaper — and those stories can be posted on your Web page, either to trigger a class discussion or to show your students some real-world exemplars of the topics you're covering in class.

184 *See* Brian Huddleston, *A Semester in Exile: Experiences and Lessons Learned During Loyola University New Orleans School of Law's Fall 2005 Hurricane Katrina Relocation*, 57 J. LEGAL EDUC. 319, 346 & n.62 (2007) ("Podcasting — recording and posting audio files on line for users to download — is much simpler [than streaming video], and most students are familiar with it.").

185 The main advantage of podcasting is that it enables students to hear your lecture more than once, and it saves absent students from missing your lecture entirely. This means that students can go back to a particular point in your lecture to confirm or clarify exactly what you said. On the whole, then, podcasts can help students better absorb the content of your lecture. But there are some drawbacks to podcasting. Since the voices and identities of *students* may be audible on a podcast, there is an important need for protecting student privacy. This may be curable by posting the audio file on a password-protected Web page and by limiting the length of time that podcasts are archived. Another drawback is that professors cannot be as unguarded in their remarks; they'll have to avoid making uncharitable asides about local judges and politicians. (Perhaps this is a *pro* and not a *con*.) Finally, podcasting might encourage students to think that they don't have to pay attention in class since they can always hear the lecture some other time. In the end, it would seem that the advantages of podcasting already outweigh the drawbacks, and that podcasting will be widely practiced once it becomes less expensive.

186 CALI has developed a project whose aim is to give law faculty a low-cost means of creating and distributing podcasts to their students. *See* CALI Classcaster, Legal Education Podcasting Project, *available at* http://www.classcaster.org/.

187 *See supra* § V(B)(3).

188 Even when a student asks a question that appears on your exam, and you provide a thorough answer, it doesn't necessarily translate into better performance by that student. Why not? Because students are processing so much information in the days leading up to the exam that they may only digest a fragment of your answer.

189 Will you issue grades solely on the basis of a final, end-of-the-semester exam? Some professors hesitate to give a mid-term exam because they worry that the students are not ready to be tested then, that the students cannot adequately digest the material in half a semester. Other professors worry that it just isn't fair to base the entire grade on a single test, covering four months of material, at a point in time when students have not yet received a single piece of written feedback. One possible solution to this problem is to give the students a *practice* midterm that does not result in a grade but does provide written feedback on how they performed. Colin Miller has posted a thoughtful blog on graded versus ungraded midterms at http://prawfsblawg.blogs.com/prawfsblawg/2009/04/the-ungraded-midterm.html#more (last visited Apr. 6, 2009).

190 When creating exams for our substantive courses, we both rely on the essay format. But within the essay format there is room for variation. In Contracts, for example, one of us creates a single fact pattern embedded with multiple issues and asks for an analysis of all the rights and duties of the parties, while the other creates a number of shorter fact patterns, each of which features a directed question (e.g., "Is there an *offer* here?").

191 For the final exam in his Evidence course, one of us creates thirty-five courtroom vignettes, each of which culminates in an objection that requires a ruling by the judge. The student plays the role of the judge, identifying the applicable rule of evidence and explaining why the objection must be sustained or overruled.

192 For the final exam in his Civil Procedure course, one of us creates an extensive background file for a hypothetical lawsuit, replete with a detailed fact pattern, the parties, the claims, the elements of those claims, geographical information about the location of the courthouse and available witnesses, potentially applicable long-arm statutes and choice-of-law rules, and some pieces of evidence, including bits of deposition testimony. He then creates twenty-five narrowly focused questions that arise at various points in the lawsuit, from the filing of the complaint to post-trial motions.

193 Fed. R. Evid. 611(c).

194 U.S. Const. amend. XIV, § 1.

195 *See, e.g.,* Lynn M. Daggett, *All of the Above: Computerized Exam Scoring of Multiple Choice Items Helps to: (A) Show How Exam Items Worked Technically, (B) Maximize Exam Fairness, (C) Justly Assign Letter Grades, and (D) Provide Feedback on Student Learning,* 57 J. Legal Educ. 391 (2007) (identifying a number of advantages to using multiple choice questions).

196 *Id.* at 392 n.2 (offering an excellent bibliography of the scholarly literature on the pros and cons of the multiple choice format).

197 *See, e.g.,* Kenney F. Hegland, *On Essay Exams,* 56 J. Legal Educ. 140 (2006) (expressing concern about the growing use of multiple choice exams in American law schools).

198 *Id.* at 141.

199 *Id.* at 140-41 (surmising that the impetus for multiple choice exams may stem from the desire of law professors to be freed from the onerous burden of *grading* essay exams, so that their time can be more "profitably" spent on scholarship).

200 Daggett, *supra* note 195, at 394-95.

201 Professor Daggett observes: "[I]n large classes I regularly use a multiple choice exam compo-
    nent (typically one fourth to one third of a three hour exam and less than half of the grade for a
    course)." *Id.* at 393. If you use a combination of essay and multiple choice on your exam, you
    may want to do a statistical analysis of the correlation in performance on the two sections or at
    least eyeball how the top and bottom students in one format do on the other format.

202 It may also be necessary to label more clearly any "majority" or "modern" or "better" rule if
    you are going to use multiple choice questions, whereas on an issue-spotting exam most profes-
    sors are happy if their students demonstrate that they can apply more than one approach.

203 The professor must take great care when wording the question to ensure that there is no ambi-
    guity about precisely what issue should be addressed. Be careful as well with the statement that
    identifies issues *not* to be addressed; students sometimes err by interpreting these statements very
    broadly.

204 One of the attractions of the directed essay question is that it makes more efficient use of the
    hours allotted for the exam. This efficiency is achieved by creating a relatively compact fact
    pattern (in contrast to the lengthy, detailed scenarios that typify a traditional essay exam), and
    by directing the student's attention to a very specific issue (in contrast to the "discuss-all-rights-
    and-duties" imperative that characterizes a traditional essay exam). You can build upon this
    efficiency by stringing together a succession of directed essay questions that are all based on a
    common fact pattern, rather than writing a whole new story for each question. Simply add a
    few new details (e.g., "Now assume that …") with each transition to the next directed question.
    This format affords efficiency yet again when it comes to *grading* the exams, since every student
    addresses the same issue in the same place.

205 For some excellent advice on creating law school exams, see SCHACHTER, *supra* note 2, at 195-
    200.

206 Be sure to establish early in the semester (preferably in the syllabus) your expectations regarding
    the content and format of your exam. Then, throughout the semester, give the students periodic
    reminders in class.

207 *See* Sparrow, *supra* note 16, at 6 (advocating the implementation of "rubrics, or detailed written
    grading criteria").

208 *See infra* § XI.

209 One weakness of a detailed point system is that it gives little or no credit for good organization
    and persuasive style. One cure for this is to explicitly award "style points" for these criteria.

210 First-year students, in particular, will write more than necessary even when correctly address-
    ing an issue, redundantly defining terms and stating rules in ways that many professors will not
    reward with points.

211 A recent study found that there is "little or no correlation" between test-taking speed and
    reasoning ability — and that the current emphasis in law schools on time-pressured exams "may
    skew measures of merit in ways that have little theoretical connection to the actual practice of
    law." William D. Henderson, *The LSAT, Law School Exams, and Meritocracy: The Surprising
    and Undertheorized Role of Test-Taking Speed*, 82 TEX. L. REV. 975, 975-76 (2004).

212 Additional time will not always lead to a proportionate increase in how much they write —
    because some of them will have already written everything they have to say regardless of how
    much extra time you give them.

213 One legitimate purpose for imposing page or word limits *might* be to prepare students for the
    essay portion of state bar exams — but the bar exam is a long way off for first-year students.

214 You need not reduce the open book/closed book question to a stark all-or-nothing choice.
    You're perfectly free to adopt an "in-between" solution. In statutory courses, for example, some

professors create a special supplement that the students must use in lieu of their own materials. To alleviate anxiety (particularly in first-year courses), some professors allow each student to bring in one index card or one sheet of paper filled with information. Other compromise positions — for example, allowing each student to bring an outline that she wholly or partly authored — invite conflicting interpretations and create policing problems.

215 This raises another argument against gut-reaction grading. It can be carried off successfully, if ever, only by grading a large number of exams at one sitting, requiring large blocks of time that are all too scarce for most professors.

216 You may want to make a few notes to yourself on the scoring sheet — e.g., "Didn't state the rule clearly," or "Confused remedy for breach of contract with remedy for promissory estoppel."

217 *See infra* § XII.